THE ELEMENTS OF
ORCHESTRAL
ARRANGEMENT

ALSO BY DR. WILLIAM LOVELOCK

Published by G. Bell and Sons, Ltd

A Concise History of Music
The Rudiments of Music
A Student's Dictionary of Music
Common Sense in Music Teaching

Published by A. Hammond and Company

Questions on the History of Music
First Year Harmony
Second Year Harmony
Third Year Harmony
The Examination Fugue
Free Counterpoint
Hints on Working Rudiments Questions
Form in Brief

THE ELEMENTS OF ORCHESTRAL ARRANGEMENT

William Lovelock, D.Mus.

LONDON

G. BELL AND SONS, LTD

MT
70
.L6

Published by
G. Bell and Sons Ltd
York House
Portugal Street
London, W.C.2

S B N 7135 0681 4
Printed in Great Britain by
William Clowes and Sons, Limited, London and Beccles

Foreword

EXAMPLE, we are told, is better than precept, and it is this morsel of traditional wisdom that I have tried to follow in planning this book.

My aim is to help the examination candidate and others who are concerned with arranging passages or pieces for orchestras of varying sizes and constitution.

This is not a book on writing for orchestra from the composer's point of view, even though it may perhaps be not unhelpful in that direction. The composer who knows his job does not write his music as it were in the abstract and then proceed to score it; he conceives it in terms of the orchestra, in a purely orchestral idiom. There is a story that somebody once remarked to Rimsky-Korsakov how beautifully he had 'scored' his 'Capriccio Espagnol'. The composer flew into a temper and shouted, 'I didn't score it—I *wrote it for orchestra!*'

We, however, are concerned with transcription from one idiom, normally that of the piano, to another, and this, mechanical though it may seem, is an art in itself.

I do not claim that my solutions to the problems dealt with are the only possible ones, but they are, I hope, both practical and musical.

Brisbane, 1966   W. L.

Contents

1. Preliminary

1. Before embarking on the study of Orchestration in any shape or form, it is essential for the student to have a thorough knowledge of Harmony and Counterpoint. This may seem an obvious statement, but it is prompted by not infrequent experience of the would-be pupil who 'wants to learn to write for orchestra' when a few simple questions prove that he barely knows (if he knows at all) how to write a simple cadence correctly. The student who cannot write a decent piece of four-part harmony has precious little chance of scoring effectively for even a small string band.

2. Counterpoint, of course, does not imply the 'strict' variety (assuming that anybody still teaches or studies that pernicious form of academic narrow-mindedness) but rather an understanding of good, interesting part-writing and the ability to put this understanding to practical use.

3. Since this book is of deliberately limited scope, it is not proposed to deal with the technique of the various instruments. This and all relevant information should be studied in some such comprehensive tome as Forsyth's 'Orchestration' (Macmillan & Co.), which is available in any good library. Intensive study of such a book is essential, but it should be supplemented as far as possible by practical acquaintance, however limited, with at least some of the instruments. Much, too, can be learned from an hour or two spent with a good player who can demonstrate how his instrument is handled, what it can do effectively and what it cannot.

4. Mental hearing, the ability to hear what one sees on paper, and to imagine the tone-qualities of the various instruments, is of vital importance and little if any progress is possible unless it is well developed. Too often one finds a student assigning a passage to an instrument to which it is not only unsuited technically but on which it will *sound* inappropriate. A fanfare-like passage will sound merely silly on a couple of flutes; a soft melody involving a lot of leger lines will be impossible on a clarinet—and if attempted is likely to sound quite horrible.

(Even recognised composers at times miscalculate badly. There is a story of the late Sir Edward Elgar reading a score by one of his eminent contemporaries and ejaculating at a certain passage, 'But, Good Lord, can't he *hear* it'll sound horrible?' Elgar's own ear was, of course, extraordinarily highly developed and it is doubtful if it ever failed him at all, even though he did write an occasional passage which may give conductor and orchestra some trouble over tonal balance.)

5.   Study of the scores of works by acknowledged masters of the orchestra, *e.g.* Tchaikovsky, Elgar, Rimsky-Korsakov, teaches one an enormous amount, and even more can be learned by following performances, whether live or recorded, with scores. In some respects the use of the gramophone is really best, since one can always stop the turntable and re-hear a passage as many times as desired. Attendance at rehearsals under good conductors is invaluable, apart from the opportunity it gives of studying how they dissect works and mould them to the interpretation they have in mind.

6.   The student should be continually trying to hear in his mind the sounds of different instruments, associating them with melodies or passages with which he is familiar. Try, for example, to hear the opening melody in the slow movement of Tchaikovsky's 5th Symphony with the proper horn tune: the C sharp minor theme in the second movement of Schubert's 'Unfinished' on the clarinet; the opening of the slow movement of Beethoven's 7th with the sombre tone of the lower strings; and so on, *ad lib*. And then, if you have a gramophone, play the passage and check the accuracy of your imagination. Try, too, mentally comparing one instrument with another, for example the clear 'white' tone of the flute's middle register with the reediness of the oboe, and that with the creamy smoothness of the clarinet.

7.   The compass of every instrument must be memorised—though admittedly one may need to look up and check that of a comparatively rarely-used instrument such as the glockenspiel. The student will find it helpful to make a chart of compasses, starting with the strings and adding to it as he begins to deal with other instruments, and to have it in front of his eyes when working. The beginner (especially if he be pianist or organist) finds it all too easy to write below the compass of even such a common instrument as the violin.

8.   A special warning may be given here regarding the use of upper registers. On many instruments, the higher we go the more difficult tone-control becomes, and fingering too. We have to bear in mind not only what is possible but also what is practical. Because the textbook says that the clarinet can ascend as far as five leger-line C above the treble stave, it does not mean that this highest range may safely be used *ad lib*.—that is, unless you deliberately want a noise like the last shriek of a lost soul. (In any case, Strauss said the last word on this matter near the end of 'Till Eulenspiegel'.)
    Similarly the horn, whose top note for normal purposes is (sounding) 3rd space C,

can reach as high as the F a 4th above. The ill-advised student, possibly having listened carefully to Strauss's 'Till', takes the horn up to this limit quite casually and probably marks it *piano*! He does not realise, what any player could tell him quickly (and probably pungently) enough, that (*a*) such a note is a considerable strain on the lips, (*b*) its effectiveness is in inverse proportion to the frequency of its use and (*c*) it can only be taken *f* or *ff* anyway.

9.   Another matter which needs careful thought is that of technical difficulty. If you have arranged for your work to be played by, say, the London Symphony Orchestra or the BBC Symphony Orchestra (not, admittedly, a very probable happening!), then you may, if you choose, write in terms of a band of virtuosi; but even so there is no need to write a lot of passages which will cause the players to curse rather than to bless you. Don't think in terms of a 'crack' orchestra—rather the reverse.

I may perhaps recall a personal experience which is to the point. Many years ago, the BBC Military Band, which contained none but first-class players, performed a work of mine. The leading clarinet had known me since I was a boy. At the end of the rehearsal he called me over and said, 'You know, young Lovelock, that was . . . . . . difficult.' This, coming from one who was acknowledged to be one of the most accomplished players in the country, shook me considerably, the more so since he knew that I had studied the clarinet to a reasonable extent and should therefore have known better. It was a salutary lesson. One should always remember that orchestral players are not keen on having to take home their parts for intensive practice.

10.   A final point of the utmost importance when arranging for orchestra is that we are dealing with musical sounds, not merely with black dots on paper. This obvious remark arises from what was said earlier with regard to mental hearing. The student must have as clear an idea as possible of what his score will sound like. (One sometimes wonders whether some of our 'contemporary' composers have any idea at all of the actual sound of what they write.) It is not a matter of transcribing one lot of notes on the printed page as another lot of the same pitch in some kind of orchestral score. The student must be continually and continuously asking himself whether what he has written is apt, playable and effective. Is this the right colour for this melody? Is my chord-spacing effective in orchestral terms? Am I writing in a truly orchestral idiom or am I merely trying to make the orchestra sound like a piano? And so on.

11.   A relevant list of the customary abbreviations is given at the beginning of each chapter which follows. They must be memorised and employed.

12.   The examples discussed are practically all from Schumann's 'Album for the Young', of which the student must have a copy at hand. All references to numbers without titles, *e.g.* No. 15, are to pieces in this book. Numbering of bars begins always from the first whole bar and repeat bars are disregarded. Access to Beethoven's piano sonatas is also necessary.

2. Strings (1)

Abbreviations: V.1. — 1st violin

               V.2. — 2nd violin

               Va. — viola

               Vc. — cello

               CB (DB) — contra basso (double bass)

               arco — with the bow

               pizz. (*pizzicato*) — plucked

               ⊓— down bow

               ᴠ— up bow

               Div. (*divisi*) — divided. One section, *e.g.* 1st violins, divided to play two separate parts. The right-hand player at each desk takes the upper part and the left-hand player the lower

               Unis. (*unisoni*) — contradicts *divisi*

               Esp. (*espressivo*) — frequently used to indicate to the player that his part is of some extra importance and must therefore be treated as expressively as possible

Compasses

1. Neatness, clarity and a good appearance in a score are essential and the student must take pains to achieve them. Normally five staves are required, and at the beginning of the first score it is usual to put the name of each instrument in full—1st violin, 2nd violin, etc. For succeeding scores the abbreviations V.1. V.2., etc., may be used.

There is no need to draw a separate barline for each stave; run right through the whole five. Don't cramp the bars; allow plenty of space for easy reading.

2. If there is a lengthy passage of *divisi*, it may be well to use two separate staves, especially if the two parts are markedly independent or if they cross. Bracket the staves at the beginning of the line. Ex. 2 (*b*) is obviously clearer than (*a*):

Ex. 2

Always remember to put *unis.* when the instruments reunite after *div.*

3. Whole-bar rests need not be inserted; even in printed scores it is becoming customary to omit them. Expression marks must be inserted in all parts, and it is usual to put them below the part concerned. The presence or absence of such markings is a pretty clear indication as to whether the student is thinking musically or otherwise, and whether he appreciates the expressive possibilities of individual melodic lines. The lack of detailed dynamic markings, and of bowing and/or phrasing, is a sure sign of an amateurish approach.

4. *Bowing.* To the non-string player this is apt to present a problem, and the best advice is to consult a competent violinist or cellist—or study a stringed instrument yourself. Bowing must, in any case, indicate clearly contrasts of *legato* and *staccato* and the basis of the desired style of phrasing—even though the leader of the orchestra may quite likely modify details. Consider the differing effects of the following:

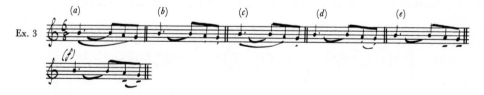

Ex. 3

The bowing suggested for any given passage will depend on (*a*) the over-all style of the piece and (*b*) the expressive requirements of the passage itself. Remember that piano composers have always been inclined to throw slurs about simply to indicate *legato*, regardless of the actual phrasing which the music itself may imply. Refer to no. 22 as a case in point—Schumann's slurs merely supplement the initial marking *sehr gebunden,* very smooth. Bars 1 and 2 could be taken under one long bow, but we must allow for the fact that the first little phrase of the melody ends on the G sharp in bar 2, the final two quavers being a kind of link to the next phrase. Hence:

The change to up bow on the A in bar 1 need not break the *legato*, and the ensuing down bow on the first note of bar 2 will provide the necessary slight stress. Down bows tend to begin more strongly than up bows.

In bar 6 the *fp*, which simply implies a strong accent, can do with a down bow. Hence, despite Schumann's slurs:

There is no need to insert ⊓ and ∨ continually; the player (or the conductor) can generally be relied on in this matter.

Detailed bowing must be indicated at all times, and this should be done as far as possible while the part is being written. Too often one has to check students for omitting bowing either partially or entirely.

5.   *Double stops and divisi*. String writing is based chiefly on four parts. When more than four are needed, *e.g.* for fuller texture, we may have to choose between double stopping on one or more instruments and *divisi*. Everything depends on the individual passage, but remember that (*a*) double stopping may cause difficulties of intonation and fingering and (*b*) dividing tends to weaken the body of the tone. Consider ex. 6:

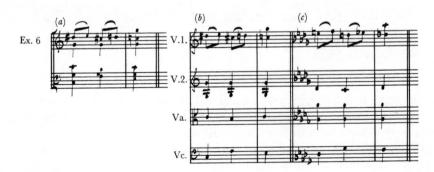

(*a*) We will assume that owing to the prevailing style it is not desirable to thin out to four parts.

(*b*) is quite simple. The lower note of the double stops on V.2 is an open string. Va. placed between the two notes of V.2 is quite satisfactory.

Transposed up a semitone into D flat major no open strings are available, but as long as we use the repeated octave double stops all should be well, whether we simply transpose (*b*) or re-arrange as at (*c*). Of course, if you are writing for players of very doubtful ability, the safest thing is to divide either V.2 or Va. and deal with tonal balance at rehearsal. From the purely practical point of view, dividing V.2 is likely to be better than dividing Va. Violas are generally in short supply.

'Casual' double stops in a moving passage are to be avoided.

Ex. 7

This sort of thing is easy enough on the piano but far from comfortable on the violin. This point is further dealt with in discussion of bar 11 of no. 22 in chapter 3.

6. In big chordal passages triple stopping may at times be needed—examples appear later. The mechanics of double and triple stopping are dealt with in detail by Forsyth, to whom the beginner should make continual reference. Better still, gain some practical experience of a stringed instrument.

7. Doubling of parts. As long as we are working on the basis of four part writing, the ordinary procedures of such writing should normally be observed. Don't double 7ths or leading notes; resolve 7ths in the orthodox manner; and so on. But in full chordal writing, involving *divisi* or double or triple stops, all that has to be watched is doubling the bass in upper parts. There are naturally inevitable exceptions, and octave doubling of Vc. by CB is always in order (see chapter 3). The following rules should normally be followed:

(i) Don't double the bass of a major first inversion. (The intelligent student need not quote Sibelius against this rule; he was a law unto himself.)

(ii) Don't double a bass leading note. (In no. 29, bars 42 and 44, one could wish, with all due respect to Schumann, that the R.H. B naturals were not there!)

(iii) Don't double a bass 7th.

Conversely, 3rds and 7ths of chords, and leading notes, may be freely doubled between upper parts always provided they are not also in the bass.

Ex. 8

This is quite acceptable. As long as you are dealing with 'traditional' harmony, resolve 7ths in the traditionally correct manner.

8.   Spacing. It is absolutely essential to keep continually in mind that in arranging for orchestra *we are transcribing from one medium and idiom to another.* What can be done on the piano is conditioned and limited by the capabilities of ten fingers and two feet. (Pianists please note the last two words. A pet saying of the great teacher Leschetizky was that 'the piano must be played with two hands and TWO feet'.) The orchestra is not limited by such a matter as hand-stretch, but there are many things which the piano can do that the orchestra cannot. For example, as Sibelius is reported to have remarked, the orchestra has no sustaining pedal so we have to create one—not that the student is recommended to try to adopt Sibelius's methods of doing so. A passage which is playable and effective on the piano may, if transcribed literally, sound quite ridiculous on the orchestra. This is apt to apply especially in the matter of spacing of chords. When Beethoven concluded a movement as at ex. 9 (*a*) he was writing in terms of the piano as it existed in the early years of the 19th century. Transcribed literally as at (*b*) the lack of well-spaced inner parts would be hopelessly weak, while the lower part of the chord would sound like a glorified grunt. It must be arranged in some such way as at (*c*).

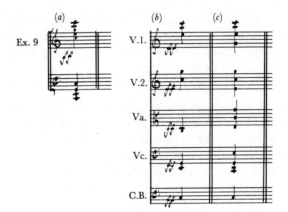

Apart from such an extreme case as this, chord spacing on the keyboard is inevitably conditioned by stretch and continually has to be recast for orchestral purposes. There are always plenty of exceptions and special cases, but at the present stage we are concerned with the general rather than with the particular. Consider ex. 10. (*a*) is perfectly effective on the piano, but on strings the lack of middle-pitch inner parts will be all too noticeable. The solution is to divide the three upper parts as at (*b*). The Vc. is left undivided so as to give a solid foundation. Note, too, the complete line of octaves on V.1; the lower A on the last quaver of bar 1 is obviously implied.

Ex. 10

Refer to no. 29, bars 16 to 20. The two hands, starting wide apart, gradually converge in a kind of 'concertina-ing' effect. Even so, literal transcription is ineffective. Hence:

Ex. 11

Note the interlocking between V.1 and V.2 and between V.2 and Va. Vc. and CB are not divided (*a*) to give a solid foundation and (*b*) to enforce the bass line which imitates the melody of the preceding four bars.

9. This last remark leads to comment on the importance of preliminary analysis, especially of thematic working. (Once again, we are dealing with music, not merely with abstract dots on paper.) The importance of texture and of the use the composer makes of thematic material must be appreciated.

Refer to no. 22. The basic melodic figure of the piece is the tune in the first bar or so. Study how it is used from bar 9 onwards (repeat of bars 1 to 8 disregarded). Bar 9, top part; bar 10, bass; bar 11, top part; bar 12, partially in bass; bar 13, inner part, coming off the dotted crotchet in bar 12; and so on. Unless this little bit of contrapuntal treatment is clearly understood, good scoring cannot be assured.

10. We will now deal in detail with no. 15. Since it lies mostly rather high we do not need the CB; a lot of low notes will mar the 'floating' effect that Schumann obviously wanted. Refer continually to the solution in ex. 14.

Bar 1. There is no need to add a fourth part; begin with V.1, Va. and Vc., V.2 entering with the A on the second quaver of bar 2.

Bars 2–3. The tie is not, one feels, essential, but it is easily managed by tying V.1 across the barline, V.2 crossing above to the melody and continuing at the top until the tie from bar 6 to bar 7. Here V.2 holds the tie and V.1 resumes the melody line.

Bar 4. Thinning out to three parts will be avoided thus:

Ex. 12

Notes: (*a*) The E sharp, leading note of F sharp minor, goes naturally to the tonic.
     (*b*) V.1 drops to B, doubling the *root*.
     (*c*) V.1 is tied across the barline to the accent. Always try to avoid ending a phrase on a long note which itself finishes up against a barline; take it round the corner to the accent so that the player knows exactly when to come off.

Bar 6. According to Schumann's notation the fourth part enters on the semiquaver D sharp. To avoid a possible bump we shall bring in the fourth instrument on the second quaver of the bar, incidentally thus adding tone to the octave G sharp which, *musically* needs something of an accent.

Bars 9–12. Much is to be learnt here.

(*a*) The arpeggio R.H. chord is purely pianistic. Orchestrally only the harp (with which we are not concerned) can do it. We now come up against the important matter of *underlying implications*. Basically bar 9 is a quaver melody with a chordal accompaniment, the implication being:

Ex. 13

The nearest thing we can get to suggesting the R.H. arpeggio is to put an octave grace note to the top A, and this will help with the marked *fp*. The doubling of the 7th (A) is quite harmless between upper parts. The two parts concerned are performing quite different functions, melody and accompaniment, and the 7th is properly resolved in the inner part.

(*b*) Bar 10. V.1 continues with the top part, V.2 taking the inner melody. But V.2 does not tie the low G sharp which is taken over by Vc. in bar 11. V.2 goes over to the accent on upper G sharp.

(*c*) Bars 11–12. Va. takes inner melody, landing easily on the A in bar 13. Note what happens to V.2.

Bars 13–14. A new melodic fragment appears (V.1) *and is repeated in an inner part in 15–16.* This latter will obviously be on Va. with Vc. on the bass. But we have to allow for the bald bare 5th on the second quaver of bar 16; there *must* be an F sharp, 3rd of the chord, somewhere. Hence the double stop on V.2, and note that the A is an open string.

Bars 17–18. The cross below the bass in bar 17 is bothersome and needs some 'cooking up'. It is here that the use of one's ears and imagination in listening to orchestral music gives the clue—see ex. 14. The *pizz.* B on the Vc. supplies the *implied* bass lightly and the *arco* continuation avoids the uncomfortable 7th leap.

Bar 35. Similar to bar 9.

Bar 36. Thin out to three parts.

Bar 37. E sharp is implied through the first three quavers. The five-part chord on the fourth quaver is purely piano spacing and is best spread out. The problem of the fifth note (C sharp) is solved by double stopping on Vc. or *divisi*.

Bars 37–38. The consecutive octaves A to B across the barline are best eliminated; adjust the part-writing.

Ex. 14

Notes: (*a*) The ties make Vc. bass sound more truly orchestral, the one long sound continuing below the moving upper parts.

(*b*) The Vc. G sharp cannot be left hanging in mid-air. Let it take its logical
progression for the cadence.

(*c*) Additional notes on V.2 give an easy lead-in to bar 12.

(*d*) Va. goes round the corner.

(*e*) The spread chord is warmer and fuller.

3. Strings (2)

1.   The Double Bass. The part is written an octave above actual pitch.

Especially in light scoring the CB should not be over-used. Much of its time is spent doubling the Vc. an octave lower, but to use it thus without intermission is comparable to playing the organ with uninterrupted 16 foot pedal tone. If you need a heavy low bass, then the CB is appropriate; but all depends on circumstances and context.

Ample use should be made of *pizz.* In *piano* it will add a little point to important notes in the bass line, sketching it in without making it sound heavy and cumbersome; in *forte* it can produce a good deal of 'bite' and solidity.

Whatever you may have read in textbooks, do not expect a five-string CB, nor ask for the E string to be tuned down to low C. Ask any player what he feels about the latter!

2.   Disentangling. Owing to pianistic lay-out it is often necessary to spend some little time disentangling parts and/or actually re-writing them to allow for what the piano cannot conveniently do, yet is really implied. For a simple example refer to no. 22, which is based on four-part writing. In bar 4, instead of two notes in each hand (as in bars 1 and 2), we begin with three in the R.H. and one in the L.H. and end with one in the R.H. and three in L.H. Why? For ease in playing. The F sharp on the last quaver of bar 3 goes to E and then to B on the bass stave; the tenor B on the last quaver of bar 3 goes up to D and then down to G sharp. (This may all seem self-evident, but it is amazing how often students fail to see it.) See ex. 19.

Less obvious is no. 26, bars 16 last beat to 18. *Note the basic melodic fragment in bar 1.* In bar 16 the R.H. thumb F apparently vanishes into thin air after the barline, as does also the whole of the L.H. dominant 7th chord. But the F is the first note of the basic tune, continued on from the L.H. F sharp in bar 17, the top part R.H. being a counter-melody. The L.H. dominant 7th chord lasts, by implication, through the first minim of bar 17. From the low D, R.H. begins again the little countermelody, but it switches to the basic tune in bar 18. The total implication is therefore:

Ex. 15

Notes: (*a*) The syncopated opening note of the basic figure is brought in.

(*b*) Whatever the instrument, the 7th must be properly resolved, hence the momentary doubling.

(*c*) Countermelody continued, but a drop of a 6th to F sharp, corresponding to the similar interval in the previous bar, would give octaves with the bass. Hence the modification.

3. Harmonic disentangling is often needed and may require a good deal of perception. On the piano, unless the piece is deliberately contrapuntal as in a fugue, we may find, for example, a 7th resolving in a different octave, or chromatic notes apparently never getting anywhere. Refer to no. 21, bar 15 onwards. In bar 15 there is an inner melody (derived from bar 1) divided between the hands. For convenience in playing the resolution of the L.H. D sharp is delayed until this melody reaches the appropriate E (L.H.). The R.H. F sharp on the last quaver of bar 15 appears out of the blue. In bar 16 the L.H. grace note D is the real bass on the second minim. The F sharp on the last beat *must* rise to G, and the F sharp on the second beat of bar 17 must do the same. The second half of bar 16 begins a high tune over a lowish accompaniment (compare ex. 13), so the R.H. thumb C's can be disregarded. Hence:

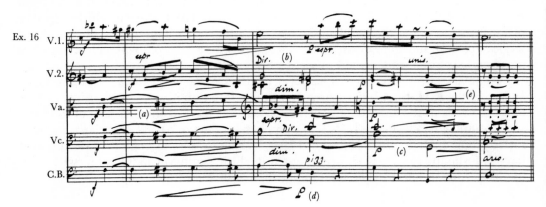

Ex. 16   V.1.
V.2.
Va.
Vc.
C.B.

Notes: (*a*) The logical progression on Va.

(*b*) The 7th is held and properly resolved. (Once again we see the vital necessity of a thorough knowledge of harmony and counterpoint.)

(*c*) Octave drop adds interest to bass line.

(*d*) Use of *pizz.* on CB, sounding an octave below Vc.

(*e*) Simple double stops on Va.—the G is an open string.

Analysis of no. 22.

Re-read what was said earlier about thematic structure.

Bar 1. The ungainly 7th leap in L.H. (Va.) is avoided by going up an octave on the fourth quaver—good string writing *versus* easy piano writing.

Bar 3.(*a*) Why did Schumann thin this out?

(*b*) What is the underlying implication?

(*a*) To make it more easily playable ('Album for the *Young*'!)

(*b*) Study ex. 17.

Ex. 17

Bar 4 was discussed in para. 2.

Bar 5 begins with a trap. The unwary student gives the V.2:

Ex. 18

which is to all intents and purposes a rhythmic impossibility. A properly developed ear tells us that the lower E is a grace note to the upper one—see ex. 19. The tie, which on the piano is the only comfortable possibility, is disregarded.

Bar 5 leads to a climax in the middle of bar 6 and in view of the strong upward tendency, culminating on a tightly spaced chromatic chord, we shall not put the bass in octaves. This climax chord needs the extra (fifth) note, easy enough as shown in ex. 19. The A sharp must take its logical progression to B.

Bar 9 presents no problem, but for variety the tune may be switched to V.2.

Bar 10, however, needs much thought. Top part is V.2, bass is Vc., but we cannot conveniently include all three of the E, D and G sharp. Schumann makes the G sharp vanish into thin air—it cannot do otherwise because of the bass line, and if we transfer it to the 'alto' part we cannot hold it because of a nasty clash with the A. Nor, indeed, can we apparently do anything else, so we must be prepared to modify into purely string terms.

There seem to be two possible solutions. (i) Omit the G sharp altogether and rely on the D to give the effect of the dominant 7th, (ii) arrange as shown in ex. 19. The latter is preferable.

Bar 11. V.1 resumes the melody. In view of the bass leap across the next barline and the imitation of the thematic rising quaver passage, it will be good to rest Vc., re-entering from the low E. But what are we to do about that four-part chord on the fifth quaver, when we have only three instruments? A 'casual' double stop on V.2 is not good, and the final chord is in any case pretty empty with no F sharp in it. The only solution is to divide V.2.

Bar 12 begins the same as bar 10. Schumann does not resolve the 7th (D) but we shall, and so modify the inner part. The accented A on the bass stave is simultaneously bass and a sort of tied anacrusis to the inner melody in bar 13 (see the reference to this passage in chapter 2). It looks, therefore, as if it should be given to Va. since its pitch is appropriate. But—and it is a big but—look ahead to bar 14 and do some disentangling. The basic figure begins again on the L.H. F sharp *and on the fifth quaver of the bar goes over to the R.H.*, returning to L.H. on the first note of bar 15. This is the kind of thing which prompted the previous remarks about texture. At least 50% of students could be relied on not to spot the point.

From all this emerges the fact that if we use Va. for the theme in bar 13 we have nothing left for its appearance in bar 14, since it is too low for V.2. Further, bar 13 is the climax so dividing a part is undesirable. The solution is to use V.2 in bar 13, saving Va. for bar 14.

Around here the CB *arco* is needed to give a solid bass and to back up the climax effect. Bar 16 is clarified by the notes on ex. 19.

Bars 21–22. The arpeggio effect must be disregarded, see ex.13. More 'cooking' is needed here in view of (*a*) the thin chord in the second half of bar 21, (*b*) the fact that the passage is really melody with chordal accompaniment, (*c*) it is a climax point and (*d*) we want if possible to get in the L.H. arpeggio. V.1 and V.2 can neatly work antiphonally. Simple double stops provide a solid enough chordal background and the CB adds 'bottom'. Note the final *arco* note (and try to imagine its effect) and the indication $>$. The CB 'fades out'.

In the second chord of bar 22 the theme appears in the 'alto' (hence the marking *esp.*). The R.H. B is really needless and if introduced will tend to cover up the entry of the theme. Conversely, a middle F sharp held across the barline gives better spacing for the start of bar 23.

Bar 23. For really good part-writing an E is needed in the R.H. on the last quaver.

Ex. 19

Notes: (a) The top E is not the open string. Low E has been taken by first finger on the D string and all the player has to do is hold it and put his fourth finger on the A string.

(b) Note the part-crossing and the 'cooking' of the Va. part.

(c) Va. goes round the corner to the accent.

(d) F sharp is implied.

(e) A double stop is needed to get the full five notes, all of which are needed. V.2 does this easily since D is an open string.

(f) Theme on Va., above V.2, gives a touch of colour.

EXERCISES

Score the following for string orchestra with double bass:
1. Schumann, no. 30.
    Notes: Bar 2 last beat, respace so as to include a tenor D.
    Bars 8–11. Some filling out is needed, with the minim melody entirely in octaves.
    Bar 13. Which instrument for the quaver inner part? Allow for what happens in bar 14.
    Bar 39. Be careful to disentangle the parts on the upper stave.
2. Schubert, Impromptu in A flat, op. 142, no. 2, up to the change of key-signature. (A good deal of re-spacing is needed in this.)
3. Schubert, Moment Musical, no. 2, in A flat, up to the change of key-signature.
4. Grieg, Lyric Pieces, op. 43, book 3, no. 3, 'In der Heimat'.
    This needs some use of *divisi* lower strings near the end.
5. Beethoven, Piano sonata, op. 2, no. 2, 2nd movement, bars 1 to 19.

4. Strings (3)

THE following matters are all of general importance and must be properly understood and fixed in the mind.

1. A melodically good bass is always essential. In writing for piano the bass may at times skip about from one octave to another (often on account of the physical limitations of the L.H.) and yet sound quite effective. On the orchestra such a procedure is undesirable.

Refer to no. 21. It is musically obvious that the pitch of the bass in the first few bars cannot be lowered, but then we are faced with the awkward 7th leap in the middle of bar 7; somehow and somewhere we have to get down to the lower octave. The best way is to drop down a diminished 8th to the A sharp in bar 6, *from the end of one phrase to the beginning of the next.*

2. A typical and instructive example of a jagged bass line occurs in no. 28. Note that the L.H. arpeggios are inner parts, not part of the real bass. As Schumann writes it, the real bass is as at ex. 20 (*a*). (Ponder the contrast between the detached notes in bars 1, 4, 5, 7 and 9 and the sustained ones elsewhere. The detached quavers give lightness; the sustained notes occur mainly at cadence points.) The only way to get a decently orchestral bass line is to modify pitch whole-heartedly as at (*b*):

Ex. 20 (*a*)

(*b*)

etc.

3. Since this piece has been mentioned it may be well to discuss its accompanimental parts, which require a good deal of management. The L.H. arpeggios need always to be taken 'round the corner' and must be modified in one or two places. In bar 3, for example, the G natural, being the bass and a 7th, should not be doubled. The arpeggios must mostly lie fairly low and so can only be on Vc., thus leaving CB on the bass line. In such a case it is well to put one desk of Vc. at the same pitch as the CB so as to give more point and clarity to the tone. The lower notes of the R.H. chords will remain as largely 'off-beat' accompaniment. Hence:

Notes: (a) The detailed dynamic markings. Many are not given by Schumann, but musical (*again!*) common sense suggests them. A good pianist would do something of the kind automatically; the orchestral player needs to be told exactly what to do.

(*b*) Vc. always goes round the corner.

(*c*) Modification of arpeggio to avoid doubled 7th.

(*d*) V.2 resolves 7th correctly.

(*e*) Bass gets up to given pitch, the break coming between phrases.

(*f*) Despite Schumann's notation the sound effect is that the little counter-melody on V.2 rises to take over the actual tune.

(*g*) D sharp on third quaver to allow V.1 to resolve his 7th (E) properly.

This piece is further dealt with in chapter 6 (exercises).

4. Reverting to basses, another point arises from bar 5 of no. 21. Vc. can take the grace note easily enough but orchestrally it will be more effective thus:

Ex. 22

5. Bass grace notes can entrap the unwary. Refer to no. 26, bar 6. The grace note C is *not* part of the melody which begins on the last crotchet of bar 4; it is the real bass, as is also the odd B flat on the last crotchet of the bar. Whatever instrument is taking the melody will *not* take these notes, which must be interpreted orchestrally as in ex. 23:

Ex. 23

Note also the implied harmony over the B flat—V7d. Upper parts will need to include an E and a G (see ex. 45).

6. Filling in of passages designed for two not-too-agile hands is sometimes needed. Refer to no. 33, bars 25–26. This *could* stand in three parts but will sound in places rather thin and the bare 4th on the fifth quaver will show up. Work out a Va. part (ex. 24 (*a*)) or alternatively think of possible implications as in ex. 24 (*b*):

Ex. 24

Note the use of '*stacc.*' to avoid writing so many *staccato* dots.

7. Many purely pianistic idioms have their recognised orchestral equivalents, but some present real problems. Refer to no. 13, bars 2 and 4. The small-note arpeggios are pure piano writing and cannot be accomplished by any orchestral instrument except the harp—that is, literally. Yet something will be lost if in scoring we omit them entirely. A possible solution is:

The use of the arpeggio signs tells the player not to pluck the strings too abruptly. Note the inclusion of the *real* bass notes F sharp and B, respectively. All that has to be watched in such a case is that the triple stops are not unplayable.

8. Turning to recognised equivalents, especially important is the kind of thing found in no. 12, bar 25 onwards. The quick alternations (a 'fingered tremolo') are not effective on strings at any speed and the accepted solution is:

This is 'bowed tremolo'.

Bars 33–36 need some filling-in, but not too thickly or the bass melody may be somewhat obscured. Note also the treatment of bars 37–40 (ex. 27):

From (*a*) the bowing on V.1 and Vc. gives rhythmic point. At (*b*) note the interlocking of V.2 and Va. on the accent. This is better than bringing in Va. after a semiquaver rest.

9. No. 29 offers another example in bars 35, 36, etc. In this case it is best to thin out to four parts for the sake of lightness—see ex. 28 (*a*). See also Beethoven's Sonata, op. 22, 1st movement, bars 16 onwards (ex. 28 (*b*)) and the Waldstein Sonata, 1st movement, bars 14 onwards. In this latter respacing of the L.H. is needed in some bars, ex. 28 (*c*).

Ex. 28

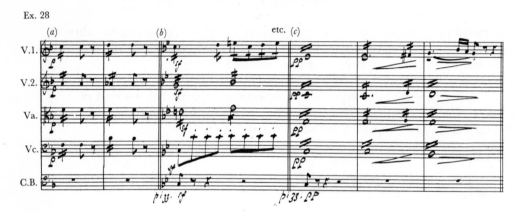

Note, incidentally, the 'string implication' of the opening of op. 22:

Ex. 29

10. Less obvious, but on similar lines and equally conventional, is the treatment of the opening of no. 23, and other corresponding passages:

Ex. 30

11. In all such cases speed must be considered. The bowed tremolo is only effective if it is fast; at a slow speed it loses its point—the 'scrubbing' becomes too marked. Refer to Beethoven's Sonata, op. 14, no. 2, 1st movement, bars 47 onwards. This is too slow for the kind of treatment discussed above, hence ex. 31 (*a*). Similarly in bar 58, etc.— ex. 31 (*b*).

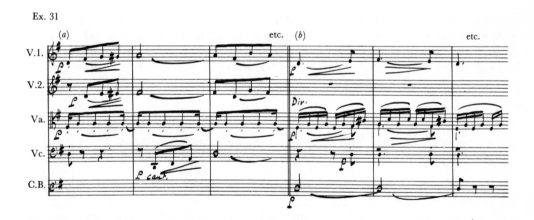

Ex. 31

The Vc. marking *cant.* is the abbreviation for *cantabile*, indicating to the player that his part is melodically important and must be sung out.

12. *Alberti basses and arpeggio basses.* There are no suitable examples in Schumann. For the former refer to Beethoven's Sonata in D major, op. 10, no. 3, last movement, bars 35 onwards. Literal transcription will sound remarkably poor. The L.H. semiquavers must be lifted in pitch and 'doubled up'. See ex. 32 overleaf.

(a) Note that Va. must come off here to avoid impossible clashes or undesirable doublings with V.1. The Vc. minims help to 'create a sustaining pedal', and the *pizz.* CB on the off-beat adds rhythmic interest. Let it yet again be stressed that we are transcribing—whole-heartedly—from one idiom to another. It is useless to try to keep to the piano figuration; think in terms of strings.

For an example of arpeggio bass refer again to op. 22, bar 4 onwards. Basically the same principle applies as in ex. 32—double up the semiquavers, *at middle pitch*. Ex. 33 (a) shows how not to do it. At the marked *Allegro con brio* V.2 and Va. would find it virtually impossible to keep the rhythm exact after the semiquaver rests. (b) is both practical and practicable. Vc. again creates the sustaining pedal.

(a) The drop to B flat here rather than to D, the proper resolution of the preceding 7th,

E flat, avoids an uncomfortable clash against E flat on V.1 on the accent. The D on Va. at (*b*) can stand since E flat is not actually *struck* against it.

13.   With regard to the rhythmic point mentioned in connection with ex. 33 (*a*), it is to be noted that speed has a strong bearing on what is or is not practicable (see also para. 11). If ex. 33 (*a*) were a steady *andante* or slower, then V.2 and Va. could manage their parts. And at any speed a passage such as:

Ex. 34

would be safe since the accented rests occur on every other beat.

As another example of this problem consider ex. 35 (*a*) from the major F Sonata of Beethoven, op. 10, no. 2. Speed is a brisk *allegro*, so either (*b*) or (*c*) would be exceedingly risky. (*d*) is the solution.

Ex. 35 (*a*)   (*b*)   (*c*)

14.   Passages in open octaves need care over balance whether for strings only or for full orchestra. Refer to no. 25, bars 8–12. Scored as at (*a*) it will sound rather empty. The middle octave needs strengthening as at (*b*).

15. One further example of basses and implications may be discussed. Refer to no. 13. Bars 2 and 4 have already been considered in para. 7. The 4th quaver of bar 1 needs a G sharp in the inner part, and that of bar 3 a C sharp—decide for yourself why Schumann omitted them. From the last quaver of bar 4 we have writing in a purely pianistic idiom which must be sorted out into proper string writing. Study ex. 37.

Ex. 37

Notes: (*a*) Complete chord at the *beginning* of the quaver pulse.

(*b*) Schumann gives F sharp and B as semiquavers, but quavers are implied.

(*c*) This bass is implied and in orchestral writing is essential.

(*d*) A handy way of avoiding either a clash of C sharp and C double-sharp, or the sudden omission of a part.

(*e*) G sharp is implied.

EXERCISES

1. Schumann, no. 13. Complete the scoring, without CB, from ex. 37.
2. Schumann, no. 17. Watch for parts which vanish into thin air and then re-appear, as at the beginning and in bar 10.
3. Grieg. Sonata, op. 7, 1st movement, bars 13 to 37 and 191 to the end.
4. Beethoven. Sonata, op. 2, no. 2, 1st movement, bars 58 to 92.
5. Beethoven. Sonata, op. 2, no. 2, 4th movement, bars 26 to 39.
6. Beethoven. Sonata, op. 2, no. 3, 4th movement, bars 29 to 45.
7. Beethoven. Sonata, op. 14, no. 1, 1st movement, bars 61 to 81.
8. Beethoven. Sonata, op. 14, no. 2, 1st movement, bars 8 to 24.
9. Beethoven. Sonata, op. 49, no. 2, 2nd movement, bars 1 to 20.

> *Notes:* (a) Orchestrally, the L.H. D in the first six bars should be taken as a series of crotchet syncopations; similarly at the repeat.
>
> (b) From the last beat of bar 12 the melody may well be in octaves.
>
> (c) Consider carefully the harmonic implication in bar 11.
>
> (d) No CB is needed.
>
> (e) Remember that the orchestra has no sustaining pedal.

5. The Wood-wind Quartet

Abbreviations: Fl. — Flute
                Ob. — Oboe
                Cl. — Clarinet
                Bn. — Bassoon

Compasses:

Ex. 38

1. Wind instrument parts are not, of course, 'bowed', but all details of articulation, *legato, staccato,* etc., must be fully marked. The tone is initiated by 'tonguing', the tongue forming 'T', or if a less marked attack is required, something more like 'D'. The notes under one slur are taken in one breath without a fresh attack, and careful consideration must be given to the exact points at which slurs should begin and end. There is a distinct difference, for example, between each of the following:

Ex. 39

The particular type of *legato* slurring used must depend on individual circumstances.
  Refer to the opening of no. 26. Ex. 40 shows two possibilities:

Ex. 40

The upper slurs are really more like string bowing and tend to break up the flow too much—too many attacks. The lower version is better. The fresh attack on the minim F will suggest a little accent, and the *tenuto* marks on the last two notes increase the expressive possibilities. There are, of course, still other ways of phrasing the passage.

2. In *non legato* passages all notes are individually tongued; the more crisp the *staccato*, the more crisp the attack. Compare the following:

Ex. 41

(*a*) will be just detached and no more, with a slight stress on the D.
(*b*) will be definitely a crisp *staccato*.
(*c*) will be mildly *staccato* with a less marked attack on each note.
Such points as these need careful consideration at all times.

3. Allow the player sufficient time for breathing. Despite Mendelssohn's version of the flute player's nightmare at the end of the 'A Midsummer Night's Dream' Scherzo, it is not advisable to write bar after bar without a single possible breathing space. Even if you don't antagonise the player, you can hardly expect him to realise fully what you have in mind, since he does not possess the in-built blowing apparatus and reservoir of an organ!

4. The Flute. Be careful how you use the lowest register as it is all too easily covered up. The 'woody' tone sounds well in a low solo passage, but any accompaniment must be very light. From 3rd space C up to about 3rd leger line E the flute is useful for melodic purposes and sings well, but remember that the tone is a little lacking in character and 'point'. (Compare it with the strongly-marked character of Ob. or Cl.) So consider well the appropriateness of its tone to whatever melody you may give it.

The top octave is bright and telling, but near the extreme of its range a proper *piano* is hardly possible.

The flute is remarkably agile, though as with all wood-wind instruments it is inadvisable to demand very high-speed work in keys with many sharps or flats. It is the normal treble of the wood-wind choir.

It can be used to double a melody at the octave above (a '4 foot' effect), but this resource should not be over-used (a common fault among organists!). Consider whether the extra brightness is or is not desirable—in other words, think of the *musical* effect. Octave doubling tends to intensify. If you do double thus a purely melodic passage, keep the accompaniment below the lower notes of the octaves. See no. 26, bars 8–12, in which the second little phrase repeats the first and so may well take the extra colour of octave doubling. See ex. 45.

5.   The Oboe. An excellent solo instrument for the right kind of melody, with plenty of tonal character. In the hands of a not-too-good player it may tend to obtrude when used as an alto in wood-wind harmony. It is useful to give extra point to an inner part in contrapuntal writing for strings and also for occasional held notes at middle or low pitch, to bind things together. Its *staccato* is always effective, with plenty of 'edge'. Be wary of the top register which, unless you are sure of a good player, may squeak.

6.   The Clarinet. This is a transposing instrument. The player always has two clarinets in his bag, one 'in B flat', one 'in A'. The former's part is written a whole tone above actual pitch so that when you write C it sounds B flat. The latter is written a minor 3rd above actual pitch—written C gives sounding A. The reason for this apparent complication is that the more sharps or flats in the key signature, the less comfortable the fingering becomes. The B flat instrument is used for flat keys, the A for sharp ones. For example, E flat major on the B flat clarinet will be written in F major, one flat. On the A clarinet the part would be in G flat or F sharp—keys not beloved of clarinettists. Conversely, E major on the B flat clarinet would appear as F sharp, whereas on the A clarinet it would be written in G—quite easy.

The clarinet can do practically anything—melodies, runs, filling in, what you will. The smooth, flowing type of melody suits its creamy tone excellently and it is useful to add a little body to a string melody.

The lowest, 'chalumeau' register has a warm, 'fat' tone with a good deal of penetrating power. Most textbooks make much of the 'break' between

but to the contemporary player it presents little difficulty except that the tone on A flat, A natural and B flat needs careful control.

In the top register the tone tends to harden and fingering becomes rather complex. Treat it with restraint and don't demand *pianissimo*—you won't get it! As mentioned in chapter 1, the clarinet can reach some notes above the compass given at the beginning of this chapter, but for normal purposes they are of little use. Always remember that on the clarinet, as on the oboe, the higher you go, the more difficult it becomes to control the tone, and the more tiring to the lips.

Many textbooks give lists of difficult or impossible shakes. Except in the highest register (where they would be precious little use anyway) they may be disregarded. On the modern Boehm instrument they present no problem.

The clarinet has a tremendous range of tone, from a piercing *ff* to an almost inaudible *pp*. It blends with almost anything and can go effectively in octaves with flutes and bassoon.

7. The Bassoon. It can reach as much as a 5th higher than the compass given at the beginning of this chapter, but only a first-class player can do this properly, so don't ask for it.

The bassoon is *not* the 'clown of the orchestra', though it can play the fool well enough when required, as in Dukas' 'L'Apprenti Sorcier'. From tenor C upwards its *cantabile* is good, with a rather plaintive colour. There is a lovely example just after letter B in the slow movement of Tchaikovsky's 4th Symphony, a perfect *locus classicus*. The 'buzz' which many people seem to take as typical only tends to develop in the bottom octave, and then only in the hands of a poorish player. For the classic example of complete effectiveness down here, listen to the opening of Tchaikovsky's 'Pathetic' Symphony.

It can add richness to a bass line on Vc. and is useful to add some edge to the CB provided it can keep within its compass.

Held notes in the tenor register are effective, as will appear in due course.

The *staccato* is sprightly and can be enormously effective in the right place. See the main theme of 'L'Apprenti Sorcier', also the solo passage starting in bar 184 of the last movement of Beethoven's 4th Symphony—though this latter is far from being a favourite with bassoonists! Avoid, however, giving the bassoon the kind of detached note bass which really belongs to Vc. or CB. A bass line such as that at the beginning of ex. 45, in that particular context, would sound quite ridiculous on the bassoon.

8. In simple quartet writing for wind quartet, the oboe generally acts as alto and the clarinet as tenor. Watch for good normal spacing. Contrapuntal writing comes off well, the four colours standing out clearly from each other. No. 34, which is entirely in four parts, can serve as an example. The student may well copy it out in the proper open score, with clarinet in B flat.

EXERCISES

Arrange for wood-wind quartet (without strings) nos. 2, 6, 11, 16.
Especially in nos. 2 and 6 note the necessity of adding an occasional fourth part in accordance with the harmony.

6. The Small Orchestra

1.   The full orchestra normally contains a pair of each wood-wind instrument; for the time being we shall content ourselves with one of each.

2.   In appropriate passages the wind quartet can contrast happily with strings, *e.g.*

On a larger scale see no. 38, where wind could take the first four bars, echoed by strings in the next four. But do not fall into the error of regarding strings and wind as simply opposing groups; don't be afraid to mix your colours. (As a young student I was supposed to be studying orchestration with a learned Doctor of Music. His advice was, 'You should have a passage on the strings, then one on the wood-wind, then the brass and so on.' The only possible comment is—! ! !)

3.   In purely chordal passages for the full band it is generally best to get wind and strings complete in themselves as far as possible, see. ex. 44 (*a*). Avoid doubling a bass progression in the middle of the harmony. In ex. 44 (*b*) the consecutive octaves between bassoon and string bass, with Va. in between, are poor.

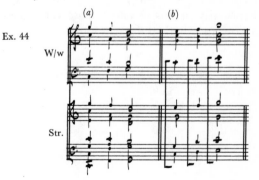

4. The wind are obviously most useful for melodic purposes. Don't be afraid to let a wind instrument take a melody entirely solo. Students sometimes seem too fond of doubling a melody needlessly on strings thus obscuring the real 'solo' colour. Let the solo be really solo.

5. In *forte* a string melody may often well be doubled by wind for extra richness and colour, but remember that strings alone are effective enough. As always, the treatment must depend on the individual circumstances and context.

6. String accompaniments to wind solos generally need to be on the light side and the CB should be used with restraint. Too few notes are better than too many.

7. With a small orchestra such as we are now considering, a climax passage needs usually to be based primarily on the strings, wind being used to strengthen and colour the various lines. It may be necessary, too, to decide where a climax actually occurs, and this can be done only through musical perceptiveness. In no. 26, for example, Schumann marks nothing above *mf* (last beat of bar 8), but musical common sense tells us that the climax of the piece begins from the last beat of bar 16, sinking down to a quiet ending from bar 19. For suitable treatment study the scoring in ex. 45.

A similar case occurs in no. 21. There is a build-up from bar 9 to bar 12, then a drop down, and the real climax begins in bar 14 leading, again, to a quiet ending.

8. In laying out a score leave a blank stave between wind and strings; this makes for ease in reading. Indicate the instruments by abbreviations at the beginning of each stave—see ex. 45, etc. Put tempo markings above the flute part and also on the spare stave above the strings. It may be worth mentioning that it is best to work on something like twenty stave MS paper—it will be needed later, anyway.

9. Analysis of no. 26, to be scored for 1 flute, 1 oboe, 1 clarinet, 1 bassoon and strings.
Bars 1–4 have a flowing melody with light accompaniment. Either ob. or clar. will serve for the melody, the accompaniment being obviously strings without CB.
Bar 2. The last beat is *not* the first inversion of the chord of G minor, but, V7d. (If you can't see this point, your knowledge of harmony is inadequate!) An E, 3rd of the chord, must be included in the accompaniment.
Bar 4 last beat begins a tenor melody, obviously bassoon.
Bar 6. Refer back to chapter 4, para. 4.
Bar 8, last beat, to bar 12. This passage, needing more warmth and fullness of tone, may well be based on strings. See also the notes at the end of ex. 45.
Bars 13 to 16 similar to 1 to 4. The solo instrument may be changed or not, as you please. But note that this opening phrase occurs again in the final two bars where a return to the original tone-colour will be appropriate—a kind of final echo of the opening. So it may

be well to change the colour in bars 13 to 16. This sort of long-term thinking, looking ahead combined with a detailed appreciation of the thematic structure, is very necessary. Bar 16 last beat to bar 18. The texture and implications of this were dealt with in chapter 3, para.2—see ex. 15. Since it is the climax, strings will be the basis with individual lines coloured by wind. Octave doubling on the flute will add to the effect, but note how it is handled in ex. 45.

Bar 19. The tenor pitch melodic fragment which begins from here naturally suggests bassoon.

Bar 20 last beat begins the final reference to the basic melodic figure.

Bar 22. The quavers can only be on bassoon. The B natural is below Va. compass, Vc. will be needed on the bass; and bassoon colour will give sufficient point.

Ex. 45

Notes: (*a*) Schumann's *fp* is replaced here and in similar places by an accent—which is all it really means.

(*b*) No need to add a fourth part to the accompaniment here; keep it light.

(*c*) Schumann's rather dissonant C is eliminated and the harmony (V7d) clarified.

(*d*) A small touch of colour on the tenor anacrusis and a fragment of counter-melody. This kind of mildly contrapuntal thinking is often productive of useful little touches which are in good orchestral style even though the original may not suggest them at all.

(*e*) Fl. at the octave adds brightness, intensifying.

(*f*) Light *pizz.* on CB adds variety and interest to the bass line.

(*g*) Three parts are ample for the accompaniment.

(*h*) Strings have everything. Wood-wind are actually supplementary but add much to the fullness of effect. Note the colouring of the basic melodic figure: Va. plus Bn., V.2 plus Ob. CB *arco* gives a solid foundation and then fades out.

(*i*) To get in all the necessary notes, V.2 must divide here. Note the movement of its lower part (and of clar.) for the sake of good part-writing and to avoid doubling the leading note A.

(*j*) Ob. tone gives point to the 7th of the chord.

(*k*) Fl. at the octave stresses the lift up to the high notes—but nothing more.

(*l*) Both Vc. and Bn. land on middle C, the former fading out as the latter increases. One tone 'dissolves' into the other. Note, too, that Vc. comes off at the accent.

Study in great detail the dynamic markings.

10. In working out a score it is best to write in first the various passages, on whatever instrument, that you can be quite sure of, especially the bass, and then build up. For example, in ex. 45, having analysed as in para. 9, write in the various solo passages—clar. bar 1, bn. bar 4, etc. Then the string accompaniment as far as bar 8. Next the strings of bars 9 to 12, plus the fl. At the climax work out first the string essentials, *i.e.* V.1, Va., Vc. and CB, and V.2 in bar 18. Complete the harmony on V.2 *div.*, then put in the wind parts. And so on. It is no use trying to work from top to bottom of the score in each bar; follow through the melodic lines and think as far as possible contrapuntally.

EXERCISES

Score for the same orchestra nos. 21, 34, 13, 28 and 35 in that order.

Notes:
No. 21. This works out much on the same lines as no. 26.

    (*a*) Refer back to chapter 4, para. 1, and chapter 3, para. 3.

    (*b*) Watch the harmonic implication on the last beats of bars 1 and 13.

    (*c*) The lay-out and the varying number of notes in the repeated quaver chords in bars 9 to 12 need consideration and the proper treatment offers a good example of transcription from piano idiom to orchestral idiom. Ex. 46 shows how it can be done. In bar 9 the notes are re-arranged to avoid tangling with the melody and to lead logically to the spacing in bar 10. In bar 11 the thickening to four and five notes is disregarded and the original rhythm retained. The double stops are all easy.

Bn. may well have some held notes at tenor pitch to bind things together, and some upper wood-wind may be added from the asterisk to enrich the little climax.

    (*d*) From the last beat of bar 12 a wind solo will naturally take over the tune, but it is well to take V.1 across the barline, as shown above, so as to resolve its 7th (F) and to end the passage on the accent. If you use fl. at the octave, let it do the same.

No. 34. Bars 1 to 4 may well be strings only, wind entering from bar 5 thus:

Ex. 47

The remainder should be scored in the same style.

No. 13. CB is not needed. Refer back to chapter 4, para. 15, ex. 37, regarding texture, etc. Ample use should be made of wind solos on some such lines as ex. 48. In appropriate cases, where the melody divides up into little scraps as here, the tossing about from one colour to another can be very effective.

Continue in similar style always watching the contrapuntal texture and the possibilities of both solos and colouring by the wind.

At (a) note the use of ties rather than dots. For the orchestral player this notation, i.e. where the sound is followed by a rest, makes for safer reading.

Ex. 48

No. 28. Refer back to chapter 4, paras. 2 and 3. With wood-wind available we may
well begin with strings alone, introducing solo Ob. at the end of bar 4. Note
this treatment of bars 7 to 10:

Ex. 49

Colouring of the countermelody in bar 8 gives it extra interest (always be on
the look-out for such possibilities) and tying its first note back into the previous
bar on the Clar. lets the colour emerge gradually. The chordal passages in bars
15 and 19 should be based on strings—generally best in such cases. The former
is the beginning of a small recapitulation and may well be on strings alone; the
latter can have some wind colour added.

The detached basses in bars 14 and 20/21 will be *pizz*. Students at times put
such things on the Bn. most inappropriately. See the final remarks on the Bn.
in para. 7 of chapter 5.

In the last bar (22) the CB is best written:

Ex. 50

It *must* hold the bass, but the low A under the final quaver will be too far away from everything else for effectiveness.

No. 35. Much is to be learnt from this.

- (*a*) Although a properly organised tune only appears in odd scraps, there is nevertheless a continuous melody *implied throughout*, and this must be deduced.

- (*b*) The broken chord accompaniment must be kept very much at middle pitch. If too high, as Schumann writes it for purely pianistic reasons in bar 3, it will be ineffective orchestrally. When necessary the chord must be shifted to a lower position—see ex. 51.

- (*c*) A sustaining pedal must be created—see V.1 and Va. in ex. 51. Note their syncopated rhythm which is suggested by the rhythm of the piano version and which also avoids stodginess.

- (*d*) Also to avoid stodginess, the Vc. does not sustain through the whole bar. The effect of the bass note is heard mentally throughout each bar, but is lightened by the rests.

- (*e*) CB *pizz.* adds a little rhythmic point, though it could be omitted.

- (*f*) Bars 19 to 22 lead up to and away from the climax. Build up the scoring appropriately. Bn. may well have some tenor pitch sustained notes here.

- (*g*) In bars 23 to 26 a nice Bn. solo an octave below the treble melody is possible here.

- (*h*) Don't be deluded by the R.H. arpeggio in bar 27. Keep the broken chord figure going on V.2.

7. The Horn

Abbreviations: Hn. — Horn
a2 — two instruments (on the same stave) to play in unison

Compass (written):

Ex. 52

1. For practical purposes the maximum compass, ex. 52 (*a*), is somewhat theoretical since the lowest notes are almost unproducible, and even around tenor C the tone tends to be a rather wobbly grunt. The top 4th, though occasionally useful, is a strain on the lips.

2. The horn is nowadays always 'in F', *i.e.* written C gives the sounding F a 5th below. The part is therefore written a perfect 5th above actual pitch.

3. Key signatures are not used. Some modern writers recommend that they should be (and there is no really logical reason why they should not), but horn players dislike them intensely. Use accidentals as necessary and watch accuracy of transposition.

4. The horn's compass is completely chromatic and with its three valves quite high-speed passages are possible, though there is no need to introduce them without good cause. (There is never any need to risk antagonising the players!)

5. The horn lies, as it were, midway between wood-wind and heavy brass, partaking, according to circumstances, of the character of either. In anything up to a reasonable *forte* the tone is round and smooth with an excellent *cantabile*. Good examples are (i) the opening of Schubert's 'Great' C major Symphony, (ii) the opening melody of the slow movement of Tchaikovsky's 5th Symphony, (iii) the second subject of the first movement of Dvořák's 'cello Concerto. The intelligent listener can spot literally scores of other good examples in orchestral works of all kinds and periods.

6. In real *f* and *ff* the tone becomes penetrating, though it never achieves the sheer brilliance of trumpets and trombones. Four horns in unison *ff*, at a high pitch, can lift the roof off, and even two can be shattering enough, *e.g.* at the opening of the second subject of Beethoven's 5th Symphony—at least under some conductors.

7.   Three- and four-part chords are effective at any level of tone.

8.   Horns are very useful for quiet background harmony; their smooth tone can be very unobtrusive and 'neutral' in colour. Single and double held notes for 'binding' are also effective, the tone being a little thicker than that of the Bn. in similar circumstances. Ex. 53, from Schubert's 2nd Moment Musical illustrates the point well. Our sustaining pedal is gently created.

Refer back to ex. 32. Although effective as it stands, it could bear a little 'backing up'. Hence:

In this case, plain held notes as in ex. 53 will sound a little stodgy. The syncopated rhythm on the Hns. gives more point and 'lets some air in'.

9.   Horns and bassoons mix well, so much so that they are at times almost indistinguishable. The next time you hear Mendelssohn's 'Italian' Symphony, listen for the opening of the trio of the minuet:

Ex. 55

There are two horns and two bassoons and you may well try to decide, without reference to the score, which instrument is playing which notes.

10.   'Stopped' notes are obtained by pushing the hand farther into the bell. This produces a muffled, 'distant' tone and is very useful in *pp* and for *lontano* effects. The marking is the word 'stopped', cancelled by 'open'. (Horn players do not normally use mutes.)

11.   A special effect (like all such things to be used with restraint) is *cuivré*, in which a stopped note is attacked with great force, producing a savage snarl. The indication is a + over the note.

12. Watch for 'typical' horn passages such as:

Ex. 56

The opening of Weber's 'Oberon' Overture is pure typical horn writing, and so is Siegfried's 'Horn call' in Wagner's 'Ring'.

13. The student should make himself familiar with the now-disused horn transpositions, in B flat, E flat, etc. (see Forsyth), since they occur in abundance in works by Mozart, Beethoven and other composers, even including Strauss.

14. The full orchestra normally contains four horns but for the present we shall use only two. Two horns are written on a single stave, which may well be isolated by a blank stave above and below it. If their parts are rhythmically independent, use up stems for the first and down stems for the second. If necessary, use two staves. If only one is to play, be careful to mark the part either 1° (1st) or 2° (2nd). If they are to play together in unison after a divided passage, remember to mark them *a*2.

15. While it is usual for the 1st horn to play the higher notes and the 2nd horn the lower ones, there is no need to confine the 1st entirely to high and the 2nd to low. Any well-trained player can cover the whole compass if necessary—he could not tackle a Mozart concerto otherwise.

16. Analysis of no. 30.
Bars 1 to 4 are repeated in 5 to 8, so the former may well be strings only, the latter introducing wind colours. The lower parts on the treble stave are well suited to horns with the tenor countermelody on bassoon.
From the second half of bar 8 we have (*a*) a slow melody (minims) which is, by implication, continuously in octaves; (*b*) a quaver countermelody; (*c*) a bass which may well proceed entirely in octaves. Some harmonic filling-in is needed in bar 9 and will naturally be continued thereafter.
Bar 12 last beat brings the climax of the piece. A good deal of doubling will be necessary and we note, again, melody and countermelody. The music dies down from bar 14. Bar 20, last beat, although nothing is marked, musical common sense suggests reinforcement of the tone.
Bars 22 to 24. The real melody seems to get tangled up with the 'alto' and so must have some clearly distinctive colour.

Ex. 57

Notes: (*a*) Although Schumann does not mark any dynamic change here, a 'lift-up'
seems to be demanded.

(*b*) Horns bind things together in the fuller scoring and add a touch of warmth.

(*c*) Bassoon's part is reasonably interesting and mixes well with the inner strings.

(*d*) Horn tone is ideal here—try to imagine it.

(*e*) The oily tone of the clar. winds about smoothly and contrasts well with horns.

(*f*) V.2 *div.* cuts down the tone for a quiet harmonic background.

(g) Although just above the normal compass, this is easily manageable.
(h) Interweaving of melody and countermelody in octaves is effective, especially
    with the contrasted colours.
(i) The plaintive oboe suits well.
(j) Va. dissolves into Bn.

(*k*) Hn. gives point to the suspension.

(*l*) The lowish sounding F on 2nd horn will add some body.
(*m*) A harmless small addition to Schumann.
(*n*) Clar. tone will sound through the opposing strings.

EXERCISES

Score for 1 fl., 1 ob., 1 clar., 1 bn., 2 hns. and strings:
  No. 9.
Also Schumann's 'Träumerei', and nos. 1, 6 and 9 of his 'Waldscenen'.

Notes:
No. 9. This suggests ample use of solo wood-wind. In bar 9 watch the melodic progression at the end of the bar.
  Bars 11 and 15 the minim D must be extended to last throughout the bar—use
  your imagination to find the reason.
  Bars 17 to 20 offer the chance of a nice cello solo on the L.H. melody, transferred
  to solo hn. from bar 21. NB. If you do this, what is the final note on the hn. in
  bar 24?
'Träumerei'. This may well be attempted without the aid of any notes, but be prepared
  to use your imagination to the limit.
'Waldscenen', no. 1. There are some good 'typical' hn. passages in this, and plenty of
  opportunity for solo wood-wind. Note the figure which appears in R.H. of bar
  8 and its further use in bars 14 to 16 and 20 to 22.
  Bars 24 to 26 need some filling in.
  Bar 28 initiates a good bn. solo ending (*on what note?*) in bar 31.
'Waldscenen', no. 6. Bar 1 needs some inner-part filling in, as do all similar passages.
  Bar 15 don't take the L.H. part too literally.
  Bars 23/24 the spacing is purely for piano—allow for this.
  Bar 25. The L.H. thematic melody cannot be allowed to vanish into thin air at
  the barline.
  Bars 35/36 note the implied countermelody in the top notes of the L.H.—a
  chance for solo hn.
  Bar 46. The triplet quaver run really needs to be all in one colour and is ideal
  for the clar. even though he may have a little trouble over taking the top end
  piano. Alternatively, fl. could take over from the D flat in second half of the bar.
  Bar 48 offers a good Vc. solo.
  Bars 52/53 resolve the minim chord properly to a quaver (or crotchet) on the
  third beat of the bar.
'Waldscenen', no. 9. Note the following treatment of the accompaniment of the first
  two bars and similar places. It must be in continuous quaver triplets. (Ask yourself why Schumann did not write it so.)

Ex. 58

The repeated chord accompaniment from bar 3 is mostly best on strings. Watch the handling of grace notes in bars 17, 18, etc.

Schumann gives little if any help over details of expression or climax points. Spend plenty of time working them out yourself.

Chopin. Prelude in B major, no. 11. Note the hidden sustained melody in this; it will need a good deal of careful thinking out.

Grieg. 'Erotik', Lyric Pieces, op. 43, book 3, no. 5.

Debussy. 'The Little Shepherd' from 'Children's Corner'. Be prepared to use your imagination.

8. Double Wood-wind

1. With double wood-wind, *i.e.* two of each instrument, a full wind chorus becomes available, which may be supplemented by horns if necessary. With octave doubling by flutes this can be quite brilliant in *forte* and has a good deal of power.

2. In arranging chordal passages for this chorus, flutes are naturally at the top and it is a good plan to interlock oboes and clarinets (see ex. 59). In this interlocking a little extra brilliance is obtained by placing 1st clarinet above 1st oboe, the former having the the more penetrating tone in *forte*. But allow for which note you want to stand out. Refer to no. 23, bar 12 last quaver *et seq.*

In a case like this the doubling up in octaves is very effective.

Notes: (*a*) Both 2nd bassoon and 2nd horn on the bass, to give a solid foundation.

(*b*) 1st oboe above 1st clarinet so that the latter has the top note of the chord, F sharp.

Similar treatment would be good in no. 31, bars 5 (3rd quaver) to 8.

3. Doubling a wood-wind instrument at the unison (indicated by *a*2) does not double the volume of tone; it merely tends to thicken the quality. This is safe enough in the right context, *e.g.* to colour a *forte* melody on strings or to strengthen a bass line with two bassoons. But as a general rule, as stated earlier, solo passages are best left properly solo. Occasional exceptions occur and there is a fine example at the beginning of Tchaikovsky's 5th Symphony where the opening tune is on two clarinets in unison. It is a notable example of the keenness of the composer's ear. One clarinet would be moderately foreboding; two, with the inevitable 'wave' between them, intensify the effect tremendously. Another good instance, with both oboe and clarinet doubled an octave apart, occurs in Sibelius's 1st Symphony, last movement, four bars after letter T.

4. The important thing to remember is that (as with any section of the orchestra) there is no need to use all you have available all the time. Especially in quiet passages, the effectiveness of an instrument is apt to be in inverse proportion to the frequency of its use.

5. Two of the same instrument in parallels or near-parallels are generally better than two different ones. The strings of 3rds in no. 36 are a case in point and the opening could be treated thus:

Ex. 60

On the other hand, contrapuntal passages are better with a different instrument on each melodic line as, for example, in the fugue of no. 40. The texture is clarified by the contrasting colours.

6. Unless the texture is unduly complicated, only a single stave is used for each pair of instruments. When only one pair is required, be specially careful to indicate which —1° or 2°. 1° normally takes the upper part in two-part writing and also most of the solo work; but always try to give 2° at least a little 'jam'. A player's attention is apt to weaken if he has nothing but dull held notes, or merely minor details. In this matter Elgar is, as in so many things, the model. (I remember once hearing the late Sir Donald Tovey remark that in an Elgar score every player feels that for most of the time he has a 'solo' part, when actually he probably has nothing of the kind.)

7. Provided that the pitch is appropriate, good homogeneous four-part writing can be achieved by combining two flutes and two clarinets or two oboes and two bassoons. If you need three-part chords, two flutes with a clarinet on the bottom line are effective, as are two oboes and a bassoon or one oboe and two bassoons. Remember, too, that the chalumeau register of the clarinet gives a warm resonant bass, rather more so than the bassoon at the same pitch.

8.   Analysis of no. 33, to be scored for double wood-wind, two horns and strings without double bass. The student is recommended to score it as well as he can in accordance with the notes below and then compare his version in detail with ex. 62. Note the persistence of the opening rhythmic figure.

Bar 1 needs filling out; the bass E persists in effect throughout the bar. Hence, on strings:

Ex. 61

Or better, the more sophisticated version in ex. 62 where the *pizz.* strings add rhythmic point.

Bar 4. The minim chord ends up against the barline. Note the orchestral version in ex. 62—in this instance it cannot be extended 'round the corner'.

Bars 4 to 6. Effective quick switching of colours is possible. Don't forget to go round the corner each time.

Bar 7. The L.H. refers, rhythmically, to bars 1 and 2. A full chord is desirable on the first beat—two horns and a bassoon.

Bar 8. Despite Schumann's notation, the semiquaver run finishes on the low E.

Bars 9 to 16 on similar lines.

Bars 17 and 18 similar to bars 1 and 2. Interlock horns and bassoons.

Bars 21 and 22 need filling in. The C sharp in bar 21 lasts in effect through to the beginning of 22, and 22 itself can be filled in a little.

Bars 23 and 24. Keep three-part chords throughout.

Bars 25 and 26, see ex. 24.

Bar 27. The full (implied) chord on strings with a wind instrument on the run.

Bar 28. As well to finish with a quaver chord 'round the corner'.

Bar 36. This is a little fanfare and so suggests brass, but all we have are two horns. Let them take the L.H. and use two clarinets for R.H.

Bars 37 and 38 need quick colour changes. L.H. suggests four horns but as we have only two, mix them with two bassoons and switch to strings for the repetition.

Bar 39. Another fanfare, going uncomfortably high for horns. Two clarinets seem to be the only solution. Take them through bar 40 to the first quaver of 41.

Bars 41 and 42. The implied harmony must be shown.

Bars 54 to 56 obviously flute solo.

Bars 56/57 may very well end on wood-wind only, though strings would be equally good.

Ex. 62

Notes: (*a*) Vc. *pizz.* gives point to bass.
         (*b*) Why not?

15

(*c*) A little filling in.
(*d*) Fl. at the octave brightens.

(e) Two oboes sound adequately snappy.
(f) Detached bowing on Vas. gives more point to the tumbling-down effect.
(g) A little 'jam' for 2°.

(*h*) Note that the full tally of accidentals is indicated in *both* horn parts. In such cases this should always be done, whether for horns or anything else.

(*i*) Note how this is filled in.

(*j*) Vc. *pizz.* adds lightness and point.
Note throughout the continual quick changes of colour which are appropriate in a piece
of this bright character.

EXERCISES

Score for double wood-wind and strings (no horns):
>No. 36.

Score for double wood-wind, 2 horns and strings:
>Nos. 37 and 39. Also, Beethoven Sonata, op. 2, no. 3, Scherzo (without Trio), Sonata, op. 2, no. 2, 2nd movement, Sonata, op. 13 ('Pathétique'), 2nd movement, and op. 31, no. 2, 2nd movement, up to bar 43.

Notes:

No. 36. Ex. 60 gives the clue to the style. Don't, obviously, confine the 3rds to wood-wind.

The simplest treatment of the L.H. is on these lines:

No. 37. Watch throughout for homogeneity of tone in chords and get what variety you can in the treatment of repeated phrases.

No. 39. The winding quavers can only be strings and may well be carried on pretty consistently in octaves except in such places as bars 7/8 and 15/16.
>In bars 3/4 and similar passages two horns are needed.
>From bar 25 a little sustaining may well be devised thus:

Do not fill in at the C major change. In the first two bars the bass solo needs to be well below the (horn) chords, and in the next two bars the big gap between the R.H. and the L.H. double drone needs to stand literally.

For the rest, use your imagination and try to think in purely orchestral terms.

Beethoven, op. 2, no. 3. Very little filling out is needed—it must be mostly *leggiero*. Full orchestra only at climax points.

Beethoven, op. 2, no. 2. The opening should be fairly obvious—two horns and a bassoon with *pizz.* bass. If you continue thus from bar 13, watch what you do in 17 to 19. The B minor melody beginning in bar 19 may well be solo clar. (or ob.) but note that the accompaniment should be on strings. The melody needs to stand out so a wood-wind accompaniment is inadvisable—a more *neutral* tone is needed for it. *Note this point.* If the accompaniment to a melody is itself highly coloured, it will tend to detract from the importance of that melody.

Beethoven, op. 13. By now, this should present no great problems. Don't forget the sustaining pedal—though without overdoing it. For example, a sustained tenor E flat in the first few bars will do a lot of good.

9. The Trumpet

Abbreviation: Tpt.

Compass (written):  Ex. 65

1. Although other pitches are occasionally encountered, the trumpet in normal use is in B flat, the part being written, as with the B flat clarinet, a tone above actual pitch, with the appropriate key-signature.

2. The extremes of the compass must be treated with reserve. Below written middle C the tone tends to deteriorate and intonation can be insecure. (A quite recent experience with a first-class trumpeter convinced me of the folly of expecting the written B flat below middle C to be attacked *piano* exactly in tune.) The upper extreme (except, apparently, in the case of highly trained Jazz players) causes some strain on the lips. The lower end is not really very useful since it can be taken more effectively by the trombone, while extremely high notes are piercing, though useful, of course, in the right context.

3. The trumpet is not necessarily merely a noise-maker (the same applies to its big brother the trombone). The opportunities for using it on a *cantabile* melody are relatively rare in the kind of arranging with which we are chiefly concerned, but it has its uses for holding notes in *piano* when some more marked colour than that of, say, the horn is desirable. A possible instance occurs in no. 24, bars 17, 2nd beat, and 18, where three repeated E's in octaves would be effective. (Though actually it would be rather needless to include trumpets in the score just for these three notes.)

4. As a general rule fanfare-ish passages, at the right pitch, may be given to the trumpet, also anything of the 'tan-tan-ta-ra' variety. (For students of Gilbert and Sullivan it may be mentioned that the ensuing 'zing-boom' comes on the percussion.) Refer to no. 25. The octaves in bars 22 and 23 *must* be on two trumpets; also, though perhaps less obviously, the repeated octave E's and C's in bars 16 to 18 and 18 to 20 respectively.

5.   Trumpets can combine well with horns in chords, but in loud passages the former should always be marked a degree lower than the latter. (This also applies with trombones. If the rest of the orchestra is *ff*, mark trumpets and trombones only *f*. The heavy brass *ff* will swamp everything else, so unless you deliberately want this to happen, watch the dynamic markings carefully.) Interlocking of trumpets and horns is generally better avoided; put trumpets on top and horns underneath.

6.   Muting the trumpet produces a pinched and rather nasal tone. It should not be over-used, but it is worth noting that if we are short of a 2nd oboe, a muted trumpet makes a handy substitute, *below* the 1st oboe.

7.   Study the following arrangement of no. 25 and the notes thereon:

Ex. 66

Notes: (*a*) The snappy tone of the oboe makes a good start.

(*b*) Horns marked *leggiero* lest they tend to be too heavy.

(*c*) Some quick colour-changes for the chopped-up little phrases.

(*d*) Fuller tone of strings on the melody for the climax.

(*e*) This will help the phrase to 'whip up' to the top B and A.

(*f*) *Pizz.* strings give the rhythm an extra kick.

(*g*) Two bassoons help out violas—the tone will mix well.

(h) Each department of the orchestra has complete harmony. The wide space between clarinets and bassoons is well filled in by horns, trumpets and violas. Octave doubling at the top adds brilliance; octave doubling in the bass gives a broader foundation.

(i) Bass gets up to given pitch. N.B. Never double a moving bass in *three* octaves, though there is no harm in doing so to a melody, as here.

(j) Implied harmony is included.

(k) We are still within the climax passage, so this is doubled-up amply.

(l) Change from clarinets and horns to oboes and bassoons drops the tone slightly.

(m) This is a purely percussive use of wood-wind, horns and lower strings—two hammer blows.

(n) The springing rhythm suggests strings, and this spring is accentuated by the *saltando* (bouncing) bowing.

(o) With strings on the accompaniment we cannot reproduce the effect at (f), but horn and bassoon have a similar idea.

EXERCISES

Score for double wood-wind, 2 horns, 2 trumpets and strings:
1. Beethoven, Sonata, op. 10, no. 3, 2nd movement, up to bar 44.
2. Beethoven, Sonata, op. 10, no. 3, 1st movement, bars 1 to 53.
3. Grieg, Poetic Tone Pictures, no. 3 (C minor).
4. Grieg, 'Norwegian Melody', Lyric Pieces, op. 12, no. 6.
5. Grieg, Nocturne, op. 54, no. 4, C major.
6. Mendelssohn, Song Without Words, no. 3.
7. Grovlez, 'Chanson du Chasseur'.

10. Trombones and Tuba

Abbreviations: Trb. or Tbn. — Trombone
B. Trb. — Bass trombone

Compasses:

Ex. 67

TENOR TROMBONE   BASS TRB.   TUBA

1. The tenor trombone is 'in B flat', *i.e.* when the tube is at its shortest length (1st position) it produces the harmonic series of B flat:
In the 2nd position the slide is extended so that we get the harmonic series of A, in the 3rd position that of A flat, and so on down to E in the 7th position. Only three fundamentals, known as pedals, are available, B flat, A and A flat, *i.e.* those of the 1st, 2nd and 3rd positions. For normal purposes they are not very useful since a little time is required to prepare the lips and the tone in any case is rasping. Except for the special effect of pedals, the lowest note, with a completely chromatic compass above it, is as shown in ex. 67.

2. The bass trombone is 'in G', its compass lying a minor 3rd below that of the tenor instrument. No pedals are possible. Even if we do use those of the tenor trombone, there is still a gap between the lowest note of the bass and the B flat pedal of the tenor.

3. Nowadays it is becoming more and more common for players to use a B flat trombone 'with rotary switch to F'. By means of this switch an extra length of tubing is brought into operation, putting the instrument into F. This means that the first position gives the harmonic series of four leger line F, Ex. 68 (though the practicable compass

Ex. 68

the second harmonic an octave higher). The 7th position gives the harmonic series of B. Unfortunately this position is unobtainable, the human arm being too short for the necessary extension, and the player stops at the 6th of which the lowest practicable note is

Ex. 69

So there is still a note missing (B natural) before we reach the first pedal of the B flat instrument.

4.   The full orchestra usually contains three trombones, which were formerly two tenors and a bass. Unless you know what instruments your players have, it is as well to adhere to this arrangement rather than to budget for the modern instrument with the rotary switch. But they may well be indicated as 1st, 2nd and 3rd. 1st and 2nd are usually on one stave, distinguished by the normal indications 1° and 2°; 3rd has a stave to itself. 1st and 2nd generally use the tenor clef unless they go inconveniently low; 3rd uses the bass.

5.   As was noted regarding the trumpet, trombones are not exclusively noise-makers, though they can drown the rest of the orchestra easily enough and should usually be marked a degree lower than other instruments. For a magnificent example of trombones going 'flat out' see the Scherzo of Elgar's 2nd Symphony, fig. 120.

This passage gives rise to comment on an important point. An inner melody stands out more clearly if its rhythm is strongly contrasted with that of its accompaniment. The trombones in the Elgar, apart from their sheer power, stand out because their rhythm and note-values are entirely different from everything else that is happening. At the other end of the dynamic scale, refer to the slow movement of the same Symphony, fig. 79. The slow-moving melody, *pp*, is on fl., Cor Anglais, cl. and hns. The accompaniment is on *pp* strings, *div.*, in off-beat groups in nine parts, to which are added off-beat crotchet chords on brass *ppp* with harp and percussion *pp*. Against this mass of sound is one solitary little oboe in triplet quavers, marked up to *mf*. Looking at the passage one would be inclined to say that the oboe would never be heard, but it is—not merely because of the dynamic marking and its slightly pungent tone, but because of its entirely independent rhythm.

6.   Purely melodic use of the trombone is not too common in the kind of work with which we are dealing, though common enough in works conceived and written purely for orchestra. Note the C major motto theme in Sibelius's 7th Symphony; also the appearance of the opening theme at the return to C major on page 38 of the miniature score of Wagner's 'Meistersinger' overture. One of the finest examples of melodic use, and all the more noteworthy on account of its originality at the time it was written, is the *pp* A flat minor passage on three trombones in the 1st movement of Schubert's 'Great' C major Symphony (miniature score page 30 *et seq.*)

7. Two- and three-part chords are effective and the two principal ways of spacing them must be noted. Especially in *piano*, wide spacing as in ex. 70 comes off well:

Ex. 70

This gives an effect of breadth and richness. Close spacing gives bite and brilliance:

Ex. 71

Note the *sfp* $<$ (an effect beloved by Sibelius). The *crescendo* up to the climax always comes off splendidly provided the balance is good. Dvořák exploits the same basic idea at the end of his 'Carnaval' overture, though starting from *ff*:

Ex. 72

This really does lift the roof off.

8. Owing to its construction and technique the trombone cannot get a true *legato*, since taking two or more notes without a fresh attack each time involves a continual *glissando* (*i.e.* slither). The nearest it can get is to tongue each note very gently and hold each its full value. Elgar (as usual) exploits this possibility in the last movement of his 2nd Symphony, fig. 136. But note how it is managed. The bass melody is given *pp legato* to bass clarinet, two bassoons, double bassoon, four horns, cellos and double basses, and the three trombones are marked *ppp legatissimo*. The trombone's lack of a true *legato* is covered up by the other instruments and the ultimate effect is of extreme but quiet richness of sound.

9. Speed of trombone passages needs care, and here consultation with an experienced player is most helpful. The trombone can be surprisingly agile provided his slide-shifts permit, but it is necessary to understand them and to be prepared to work them out in detail. This kind of thing is impracticable at any speed on the tenor instrument:

Ex. 73

The B flat can only be taken in the first position, the C flat (B natural) in the seventh. On the other hand, refer again to Elgar's 2nd Symphony, Scherzo, eight bars after fig. 134. The speed is *Presto*, ♩. = 108, and the trombones are given this:

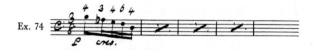

The figures show the positions. Not altogether easy, perhaps, but by no means impossible.

10. Trombones are, of course, the bass of the trumpets and full four- and five-part harmony is therefore possible with homogeneous colour, whether in *p* or *f*. But remember that it is not necessary to use them all at any given time.

11. The tuba serves as the ultimate bass to the brass though it is really not entirely satisfactory since its tone lacks the bite and brilliance of the trombones. But unless we can obtain Wagner's double bass trombone as in the 'Ring' (which is highly improbable) it is the best available. On modern instruments one or two notes can be obtained below the compass given in ex. 67, but they are not very effective.

12. The tuba can be used as the actual bass or can double it an octave below the 3rd trombone. In the former case, be very chary of putting the bass trombone on the 3rd of a root position triad—it is liable to overbalance. It can also be used independently either as a solo instrument or to thicken a bass line on double basses. As a soloist, care must obviously be taken that the melody concerned is really suitable to its 'tubby' tone; it can all too easily sound ill-advised, even comic. One of the finest examples of melodic use, where the melody happens also to be the bass, occurs in the 'Meistersinger' overture at the place where the three main themes are combined (miniature score, page 40). The fat tone combined with that of the bassoons and double basses brings out excellently the pot-bellied pomposity of the learned Meistersingers.

13. The tuba, being a valved instrument, can be comfortably agile when necessary. Dynamic range is considerable, but especially in *piano* allow for its individual tone-quality.

14. Before dealing with examples using trombones and tuba it will be well to consider the more usual percussion instruments, in the next chapter.

11. Percussion

1. *Timpani* (abb. Timp.) As with trombones, the way in which one writes for timpani depends on what are available. The usual method was formerly to write for two or three, their compasses being:

Ex. 75

If only two were available, their compasses would be (*a*) and (*c*).

2. The tuning of the timpani is indicated at the beginning of their stave either by note-names or by the notes themselves, *e.g.* 'Timpani in F, D, E', or

Ex. 76   Timpani

3. Changes of tuning are indicated by, *e.g.* 'Change F to A' followed by a reminder in notation of the notes now available, *i.e.*:

Ex. 77   Change F to A

Adequate time must be allowed for the re-tuning, say a dozen bars or so of moderate time.

4. The old, completely hand-tuned timpani are now being ousted by pedal timpani. The compass of each of the three drums is as above, but tuning changes are effected by means of a pedal which tightens or slackens the head, so that changes can be made at high speed. A *glissando* effect is also possible by gradually depressing or releasing the pedal, but this is very much of a special effect, and is, of course, limited to a 5th above the lowest note of the drum concerned.

5. The roll is indicated by the sign *tr* ⌢⌢⌢. In the case of a roll extending over a number of bars, distinguish between (*a*) and (*b*):

Ex. 78

In the case of (*a*) the ties show that the roll is to be unbroken. At (*b*) a fresh attack will be made at the beginning of each bar.

6. Single short notes can be used to point the rhythm, either with or without Vc. and/or CB. The opening of no. 29 could (*not* must) have this part for the timpani:

Ex. 79

Note that *mf* would suffice against the *f* of the other instruments.
Accents and *sforzandos* can be enforced by single strokes or by using the side-drum idioms known as the Flam (*a*) and the Drag (*b*).

Ex. 80

In no. 29 the climax *sf* in bar 17 could be marked on the timpani by:

Ex. 81

7. As a rule the timpani should sound the bass note of the chord whenever possible, but tuning may make this impracticable. In such a case let it take whatever note it has available which fits, but be wary of giving it the 7th of a chord unless in the bass. Consider no. 29, bars 17 to 20, timpani tuned, for the sake of argument, to G, A, D. Ex. 82 shows the solution if we want timpani on every beat. Actually this would be overdoing it badly, but the example should make the point clear.

Ex. 82

ORCH.

TIMP.

8. A *piano* roll on a pedal note can be very effective. See no. 23, bars 46 to 52, where it could be used *pp* on the bass D, together with a sustained note on CB.

9. Be careful not to mark timpani too high in the dynamic scale; a really *ff* roll can almost drown even the heavy brass.

10. A special effect which has its occasional uses is to play with side drum sticks instead of the usual felt-headed ones. This adds some edge to the sound, a kind of 'shrrrr'. Possibly the finest example is found in variation 13 of Elgar's 'Enigma'.

11. The *Side Drum* (abb. S.D.) The part is written on a treble stave as 3rd space C. Pitch is, of course, indefinite.

12. Even more than the timpani, the side drum's hard dry tone is useful to give rhythmic point, whether in *f* or *p*. Refer again to the opening of no. 29. Timpani, as shown in ex. 79, would be a possibility if no side drum is available; but far better would be the side drum part shown in ex. 89.

13. The roll may be indicated by *tr* ⎯⎯⎯ or by:

Ex. 83

Be careful to show exactly where a roll is intended to finish, *e.g.* (*a*) rather than (*b*):

Ex. 84

14. A *crescendo* roll from *p* or *pp* to *f* or *ff* is tremendously effective in the right context and helps to 'lift' a passage to its climax. No. 29, bars 13 to 16, shows a possibility (though not a necessity) of this. See ex. 90, bars 14 to 16.

15. *Cymbals* (abb. Cym.). The part is written on a treble stave in the top space. In *forte* a cymbal clash tops off a climax well, but above all *avoid over-use*. There is an example of such over-use (with all due respect to the composer) in Sibelius's 'Finlandia' at letter N. Unless the conductor is particularly careful this can degenerate into a merely vulgar noise. The converse is seen in Wagner's restraint in the 'Meistersinger' overture where, despite the general tendency to the rumbustious, there are exactly two cymbal clashes, both near the end, both at climax points, and both marked *f* against the *ff* of the rest of the orchestra.

16. *Piano* clashes are effective as touches of colour but, again, do not over-use. See the 3rd movement of Rachmaninoff's C minor Piano Concerto, fig. 32—of which a perceptive fellow-student remarked to the writer many years ago, 'It makes a lovely "shing-shing".'

17.   In using the clash make it clear whether you want it short or otherwise. For a short clash the player damps the sound by pressing the cymbals against his chest. Write it as a short-value note and, if you like add the word '*sec*'. If you want the sound to hang on indefinitely, *i.e.* until it dies away naturally, use what some people call the 'French slur' (bar 3 of ex. 85).

Ex. 85

18.   A roll with Timp. or S.D. sticks can be effective, especially in *p* or *p cres*. Indicate either 'Timp. sticks' or 'S.D. sticks'. The latter gives a harder, more brittle sound. After a roll, indicate the return to the normal method of playing by the word 'clash' at the next entry.

19.   The *Bass Drum* (abb. B.D.) As with cymbals, don't over-use, unless you deliberately want an effect like a brass band on the march. The low boom of a single stroke in *p*, or the 'distant thunder' rumble of a roll, can be useful, *in moderation*, but too much *forte* bass drum becomes an irritation to the ear. Write the part in the bottom space of the treble stave and indicate rolls as on the side drum.

20.   For economic reasons it is a good plan to demand only two percussion players, one for timpani and one for everything else. The latter's part is written on a single treble stave, and he must obviously be allowed adequate time to change from one instrument to another. Notate each instrument in a different space, as explained above, and indicate each instrument at its entry by the usual abbreviation. See exx. 89 and 90. The use of a single player is also a safeguard against over-use of percussion—a point which must always be borne in mind.

21.   The bass drum generally has a cymbal attached to its top, so that by using one hand for the drum and the other for the top half of the cymbals, both instruments can be played simultaneously, or in quick alternation, by one player.

12. The Full Orchestra

1. The full orchestra usually contains four horns, written on two staves. It is customary for 1st and 3rd to take the higher notes, 2nd and 4th the lower, so that a four-part chord will appear thus:

Ex. 86

1. 2.
Hns.
3. 4.

This is a survival from the days when the horn players were trained either for the high register or for the low. Nowadays any decent player can manage both extremes adequately.

2. Because you have four horns to play with, it is not necessary to use them all every time you need horn tone. As often as not only one or two are needed for 'binding'; don't thicken unduly. (The same, of course, applies in all departments of the orchestra.) In a piece of any length try to give each player his portion of 'jam', however brief.

3. Three- and four-part horn chords are effective. For an example see the opening theme of the 'Valse des Fleurs' in Tchaikovsky's 'Casse Noisette' suite.

4. Some general matters may well be noted before proceeding to dissect the scoring of a piece for full orchestra.

(*a*) Be careful not to 'use up' an instrument which you may need shortly for a solo passage. See ex. 45 where the clarinet rests in bars 19 and 20 so that its tone comes in freshly at the final solo.

(*b*) Never over-score. Even in a *ff* passage there is no need to use everything all the time, especially the brass. The student may well study the use of trumpets and trombones between figs. 3 and 4 in the 1st movement of Elgar's 1st Symphony. The players have time to breathe—and so have the listeners.

(c) On this matter of over-scoring, somebody once made a comparison between Strauss and Mozart. Strauss sits down at his desk, opens his MS score, picks up his pen and says, 'Now, how many more notes can I put in?' Mozart, in the same situation, says, 'Where's the india-rubber?' This is certainly not factual but it is a valid enough comparison, all the more remarkable, perhaps, since Strauss was known as a superb conductor of Mozart.

It is admittedly tempting (and incidentally great fun) to write for a huge orchestra, and this in itself is an equal temptation to over-score. But the real reason for employing enormous forces—triple wood-wind (or more!), eight horns, five trumpets, etc.—is not simply to make extra noise or to be able to overload MS paper with notes, but rather to have available extra tone-colours and extra resources such as three-part chords in a single wind colour. A chord on three flutes is obviously more homogeneous than on two flutes with a clarinet at the bottom; a bass clarinet below two clarinets gives greater homogeneity than a bassoon; and the use of a Cor Anglais makes available another tone-colour, as does also the bass clarinet in the low register below the ordinary instrument. The snag, of course, is economic. The more players you demand, the more that has to be paid out in fees.

At the same time, the scale of a work inevitably affects to some extent the size of the orchestra. Strauss's 'Heldenleben' or Wagner's 'Götterdämmerung' just could not have been achieved without large forces. But it has to be admitted that Beethoven managed to think on a large enough scale (not merely length) in the 'Eroica' Symphony without even needing trombones.

In any case, economy of means is always to be desired and for examples of this Mendelssohn and Tchaikovsky are as good as any. Tchaikovsky, in his symphonies, is quite modest in his demands, yet he manages to achieve far more than some composers who think always in terms of mammoth orchestras. If you are tempted to add more notes just to make your score look pretty or complicated, to double a melody which is already quite satisfactory as it stands, to demand, say, a tenor tuba when you have not written anything specifically designed for it, think again. Copy Mendelssohn or Tchaikovsky.

5. After which somewhat lengthy dose of 'precept' we will now turn to 'example' by an analysis of no. 23, to be scored for 2 fl., 2 ob., 2 cl., 2 bn., 4 hns., 2 tpts., 3 trb., tuba, timp., percussion and strings. Refer continually to ex. 89 and realise, once again, that we are dealing with an expressive and atmospheric piece of music, not merely black dots.
Bars 1 and 2. See ex. 29.
Bars 3 and 4. These can continue on strings, but the type of passage rather suggests horn tone. The lower octave, however, would be a little muddy, so prefer 2 bassoons.
Bars 5 to 8 similar to 1 to 4.
Bars 9 to 12. The *ff* fanfare effect obviously demands heavy brass, but *not* with the given

L.H. spacing. This is none too pleasant on the piano; on brass, transcribed literally, it would sound positively horrible. The scoring must be based on:

Ex. 87

The passage in doubled 3rds (top stave) must be clearly defined. Note the rests. To use full dotted crotchet chords would sound elephantine. In big chordal passages it is generally desirable to shorten the brass chords—'let some air in'. To the skeleton given in ex. 87 may be added short 'ripped' chords on strings—a percussive effect which adds tremendous punch. Wood-wind are saved for bars 13 to 16—see ex. 59.

Bars 17 to 24 similar to 1 to 8.

Bars 24/25, a B natural may well be added across the barline—compare bars 8/9.

Bars 25 to 32 are an echo of 9 to 16, but we can hardly use brass for 25 to 28 so strings must carry on. Note how the repeated D's (obviously horns) in 26 and 28 are carried across the barline.

Bars 29 to 31 may well use wood-wind colour to match 13 to 15.

Bar 33, stopped horns echo the two clarinets of bar 31.

Bar 32. Timpani give exactly the right tone—try to imagine the effect. Ditto in bar 34.

Bars 35 to 38. Pitch of bass changes from bar to bar, too quickly to continue with timp., so Vc. and CB take over.

Bars 38 to 40. Note the hidden melody in octaves. Bassoon's hollow tone will suit the expressive need. Timp. *pp* gives a low rumble in the bass.

Bars 40/41 smooth strings.

Bars 42 to 44 again a hidden melody.

Bars 46 to 52 seem to want three horns, but we must allow for what happens in 52 (see below). Hence, 46 to 48 horns, then strings. The low dotted crotchets in the L.H. can stand literally; they look muddy, but this is the effect required. For the ultimate authority for this, refer to the last eight bars of Wagner's 'Siegfried Idyll'.

Bar 52 needs very careful disentangling. If you play it accurately on the piano, you should hear:

Ex. 88

and this is what Schumann really had in mind. (If you can't follow this, your ear and your imagination need a lot of development.)

By far the best thing for the sustained A and F sharp is two clarinets *dimin.* This is almost a 'stock dodge' in such a case. See Elgar's 1st Symphony, end of 1st movement. The part on the lower stave of ex. 88 is an obvious 'horn call' and since we need the effect of dying away in the distance, horns will be stopped.

Bar 54. The bottom D is below any possible compass, but a tap on the Timp. will give something of its effect.

Note, in detail, how the score is laid out in ex. 89.

Notes: (*a*) Interlocking of wind and strings.

(*b*) 4th hn. can be dispensed with if desired—the harmony is complete without it.

(*c*) A very distant rumble adding a little colour.

(*d*) Trumpets and two trombones move up in tight parallel 3rds; horns fill in the missing notes for complete harmony. Note that in such cases two horns are approximately equivalent to one trumpet or trombone, hence the doubling of horns 1 and 3, and 2 and 4.

(*e*) Vns. and Vas. rip across triple stops. V.1 does not follow the D–E–F sharp top part otherwise its triple stops would go uncomfortably high for safety.

(*f*) Tpt. and trb. interlock the phrases—their natural rhythmic progression is *to the accent*—compare previous note on bars 26 and 28.

(*g*) This addition to the original is cribbed from the L.H. of bars 29 and 30, which are a long-distance echo of this passage. The thick off-beat *pizz.* adds rhythmic bite.

(*h*) 3rd hn. reinforces the melody on 1st hn. for the climax of the phrase.

(*i*) Tpts. add a touch of bright colour.

(*j*) Not essential but quite effective.

(*k*) This is better without the implied octaves. The single notes are a match for the preceding timpani taps.

(*l*) Ponder carefully how this and the following bassoon passage are derived from the piano version.

(*m*) The slight 'shrrrr' is worth while but not essential.

(*n*) Think out why the parts are arranged thus.

(*o*) The big gap between bass and upper parts should not be filled in or the right effect will be lost.

(*p*) *Niente*—nothing. The tone dies away to a mere shred.

Ex. 89

30

35

As already suggested, some of the percussion work is by no means essential, but it shows legitimate and effective possibilities. If, however, you are not able to rely entirely on your mental ear, it is safer to omit such effects as those at (*j*) or (*m*). Similarly with the tpt. at (*i*). Points such as these cannot be called over-scoring since they add colour-interest. Actually, there is no use of the completely full orchestra in the whole piece, and even a casual glance at the score shows how economical it is.

6.   Turn now to no. 29. Its solid chordal style presents an entirely different set of problems and the temptation to over-score must be firmly resisted.

Bars 1 to 5 need solid strings—and remember that strings alone can produce a big mass of tone.

Bars 5 to 8 need some building up and 9 to 12 still more. The temptation is to add too many instruments all at once. The build-up needs to be gradual, the second one stronger than the first and we must allow for (i) the melodic aspect of the bass line and (ii) the still bigger build-up which will be needed after the double-bar.

Bars 13 to 16. Schumann's expression marks are not very helpful, but musical common sense suggests a build-up to the climax chord on the first beat of bar 16. Inner parts must be filled in.

Bars 17 to 20. Here we can at last use the full orchestra. The melody can go in three octaves on wood-wind and upper strings with brass chords accompanying it. There must be plenty of power on the (*melodic*) bass which derives from the tune of the preceding bars.

Note especially that it is not desirable to put the 1st tpt. on the melody—it will be unduly high and strident. This kind of passage needs full brass chords with 1st tpt. only moderately high; the instruments assigned to the melody will be quite strong enough. Ample examples of this kind are to be found in standard works. See, *e.g.* Tchaikovsky's 'Pathetic' Symphony, 3rd movement, letter EE.

Refer to ex. 90. Note the use of percussion and try to decide why it is used thus.

Bars 20 to 28 similar to 1 to 8.

Bars 28 to 30 suggest a brass fanfare and here the trumpets can go right up. The importance of the dotted-note figure on the second beat of bar 29 must be realised and clearly shown. Hence the doubling up in three octaves and the use of four horns in unison. Ex. 90 (*B*).

Bars 33/34 and similar passages. There is no need to thicken the second of the two chords as Schumann does. Five or six notes are adequate—ex. 90 (*C*).

Bars 35/36, etc., see ex. 27 (*A*).

Bars 41 to 48 need full orchestra with octave doubling above and inner parts filled in. Recall the remark in chapter 2, para. 7, about doubling bass leading-notes. Ex. 90 (*d*). Note that since this is purely chordal, each department of the orchestra (wood-wind, brass, strings) has complete harmony in itself.

Bar 90 needs comprehensive re-spacing which the student may well work out for himself.

Bars 91/92. Apply some orchestral imagination and realise that this will be much more effective as shown in ex. 90 (*E*), which gives greater feeling of mounting excitement.

Bar 94 obviously wood-wind—it really derives from bars 33/34.

Bars 97 to 100. Imagination is again needed to deduce the true orchestral implication. There is a brass 'tan-ta-ra' effect to be extracted. Hence ex. 90 (*F*).

Bars 102/103 watch balance; it is easy to make things top-heavy.

Ex. 90 gives only the salient points; the student should complete the scoring on the lines suggested. See page 102 et seq.

Notes: (*a*) Timp. and S.D. not essential but help to mark the rhythm.

(*b*) A *small* addition, leading to a stronger one at (*d*).

(*c*) These 'point' the syncopation.

(*d*) Octave doubling gives a lift-up to the cadence.

(*e*) Tuba helps to fatten out CB on bottom octave.

(*f*) Gradual additions to help out the *crescendo*. Note the *short* horn chords.

(*g*) Full orchestra for the climax phrase. Melody on upper wood-wind and strings, harmony on brass. Note the arrangement of tpts. and trb. with horns just filling in. Actually, horns could be dispensed with, but it would feel a bit unfair to omit them at a big climax.

(*h*) Although it should be obvious enough, it may be worth while to draw attention to this *held* F on 1st trb. Schumann's bare 4th above the bass in bar 30 is simply pianistic convenience—the F is implied.

(*i*) Brass, percussion and lower strings provide two solid hammer-blows on the cadence.

(*j*) Oboe can be replaced by flute if you prefer a smoother tone—as in the text two bars.

(*k*) Note the complete harmony in each department.

(*l*) A quick flash of bright colour.

(*m*) Addition of V.2 *div.* (i) to strengthen Va. on the lower octave, (ii) to assist the *crescendo*.

(*n*) The close-spaced trb. bark effectively.

EXERCISES

1. Complete the scoring of no. 29.

2. Score, for same orchestra, no. 31.

   Note: (i) Watch the almost inevitable tendency to over-score. Cut down Schumann's dynamics at times.

   (ii) Despite the remark in chapter 6, para. 2, this is a case where block contrasts of tone are appropriate.

   (iii) Ample use of octave doubling is needed in places.

3. Brahms, Sonata, op. 1 in C major, 1st movement, bars 1 to 17, and 3rd movement, bars 1 to 52.

4. Brahms, Sonata, op. 5 in F minor, 4th movement (Intermezzo) complete, and 5th movement, bars 1 to 38.

13. Other Wind Instruments. The Harp

1. The *Piccolo* (abb. Picc.) is the Piccolo Flauto, *i.e.* the little flute, though its usual Italian name is Ottavino.

Compass (written):   Ex. 91

sounding an octave higher.

2. If only two flutes are available, it is useful to let 2° double with piccolo, ensuring, of course, that he always has ample time to put down one instrument and pick up the other. If three players are available, 3° will double with piccolo.

3. The piccolo is primarily for use in the high register, either to top off two flutes or to go into the octave above their compass. Never overlook the shrillness of its tone in *forte*—it can become wearing, not to say irritating. Melodically it is not often of much use, but there is an excellent example in Elgar's 'Enigma' at fig. 32. The upper part goes into the very top register of the flute, at which level and in this context the latter instrument would be too shrill. The piccolo sounds like a rather thinner-toned flute.

4. Quick runs up to climax notes are at times useful (see ex. 109), coming off well in octaves, 3rds or 6ths with flute, and a big kick can be given to a *sf* chord by using a couple of grace notes, *e.g.*:

Ex. 92

For the rest, use much discretion.

5. The *Cor Anglais* (abb. C.A. or Cor Ang.), as has been remarked by many writers, is neither English nor is it a horn. It is an alto oboe pitched a perfect 5th below that instrument and written a 5th above actual pitch.
Compass (written):

Ex. 93

6. The Cor Anglais is primarily a melodic instrument, carrying the double-reed tone of the oboe down an extra diminished 5th, though with a characteristic rather plaintive tone of its own. It blends perfectly in three-part chords with the usual two oboes and can, if necessary, be as agile as they are. The classic examples of its melodic use are Sibelius's 'Swan of Tuonela' and the slow movement of Franck's Symphony.

7. When only two players are available, 2nd oboe can change to C.A. when necessary.

8. The *Bass Clarinet* (abb. B.Cl.).
Compass (written):

Ex. 94

It is in B flat and the part is best written a major 9th above actual pitch, so that its three leger line bottom E actually sounds:

Ex. 95

Technique is similar to that of the ordinary clarinet but the high register is of no particular use since the instrument's primary function is to carry the clarinet tone down an extra octave. Many bass clarinets now have an extra key to produce the low written E flat, sounding D flat/C sharp, so bringing it in line with the lowest note of the A clarinet.

9. The tone in the lowest octave is a great asset both for low solo work, when it can sound eerie and foreboding (there are some lovely instances in Wagner's 'Ring') and to enrich a bass line. This latter it can often do more effectively than a bassoon.

10. 2nd clarinet may well change to B.Cl. when needed (but make sure that the player has the larger instrument available). Be careful to give plenty of time to make the change, the more so since the B.Cl. is rather cumbersome.

11. The *Double Bassoon* (abb. D.Bn. or C.Fag.—Contra Fagotto).
Compass:

Ex. 96   sounding an octave lower.

It is little use writing a part for the double bassoon unless you are sure in advance of its availability; it is a very cumbersome affair, found only in large orchestras.

12.   Like the B.Cl. it is useful chiefly in its lowest register, extending the bassoon tone down to the depths. Agility is poor. It has its uses to add some edge to the double basses when below ordinary bassoon compass, but allow for the noticeable 'buzz' in its tone. The classic example of its use as a solo instrument occurs in Dukas' 'L'Apprenti Sorcier', miniature score page 50, fig. 42. Its fat and fruity tone on a bass line is well displayed in the theme of Brahms's 'Haydn' Variations.

13.   The *Saxophone*. There is no need to despise this instrument, despite its association with the dance band and the peculiar brand of tone which dance-band players so often seem to favour. Well played it can add a useful solo colour to the orchestra (see, *e.g.* Ravel's 'Bolero', which requires sopranino, soprano and tenor) and has its uses as a substitute for the horn. Indeed, there are times when its tone in the middle register is almost indistinguishable from that of the type of horn now used by most players or, for that matter, from the bassoon.

14.   The seven instruments in the complete family of saxophones, from sopranino to contra bass, all have the same written compass, viz.:

Ex. 97

though some players can manage a few notes higher. Not that these extreme notes are of any great musical use since on the lower-pitched instruments they can better be transferred to a higher one, while on the higher instruments the tone tends to be an offence to the ear. The contra bass, by the way, is a rarity.

15.   All saxophones are transposing instruments. Sopranino, alto and baritone are in E flat, soprano, tenor and bass in B flat. Sopranino is written a minor 3rd below actual pitch, alto a major 6th above, baritone a major 13th above. Soprano is written a major 2nd above actual pitch (like the B flat clarinet), tenor a major 9th and bass a major 16th (*i.e.* two octaves plus a major 2nd).

16.   The alto is the most useful of the series and the one most likely to be available. It is highly agile, has a good cantabile and also has value for quiet sustained background notes.

17.   The *Harp* (abb. Hp.).   *Compass:*

Ex. 98

The composer's (and arranger's) continual complaint is that the harp is not chromatic, and although attempts have been made, nobody has yet managed to invent one that is practically so. Apart from close study of Forsyth or of a book specifically on harp technique, the only useful way to find out how it is played is to pick the brains of a competent harpist. It is all too easy to demand pedal changes which are physically impossible in the time available and (speaking from bitter experience) if the player misses a change it may be some time before he can correct it, with consequent disastrous results to the harmony. So above all, allow ample time; do not expect the player to have the foot technique of an accomplished tap dancer.

18.   Harp notation is apt to look fearsome to anyone but a harpist since it has often to rely on enharmonics. Double sharps and double flats do not exist for the harp player, so that such a chord as (*a*) below might have to be played as at (*b*). (*c*) is, of course, a possibility, but if the context were solidly C sharp minor and there were but little time for pedal changes, it would almost certainly be too far removed from the basic scale.

Ex. 99   (*a*)   (*b*)   (*c*)

19.   If the harp part can be written in an enharmonic flat key rather than in a sharp one, so much the better, since it gives more open strings. G flat major is much more to the harpist's taste than F sharp, D flat than C sharp and C flat than B. Flat keys are good if there are modulations to the sharp side—flat strings will be shortened a semitone to natural. But if modulations are to the flat side, the thoughtful student should be able to realise what complications may arise.

20.   This matter of enharmonics is really best left to the discretion of the player; the non-harpist who tries continually to work out the kind of thing shown in ex. 99 (*b*) is likely to find himself landed with some outsize headaches and may be inclined to give up in despair. A harpist recently remarked to the writer that he was sick and tired of having to 'edit' harp parts by composers who tried to be helpful. In other words, he would prefer to see ex. 99 (*a*) and arrange enharmonics to suit his own convenience.

21.   The 'setting' of the strings should be indicated at the beginning of the part, *e.g.* C♯, D♯, E♮, F♯, G♯, A♮, B♯ for the key of C sharp minor. For a major key it is simplest to indicate, *e.g.* 'Set for A flat major'. Subsequent pedal changes are shown in advance, *e.g.* D♮, B♮.

22.   Since the harpist does not use his little finger, chords cannot contain more than four notes in each hand, though they can be spaced out into 10ths well enough. (At the end of Wagner's 'Rheingold' there is famous passage for six harps, each with five-note arpeggios in each hand. The story goes that when the players complained, at rehearsal, of impossibilities, Wagner's reply was, 'Yes, yes, gentlemen—but you know what I want.' In this matter, at least, it is inadvisable to emulate the master.)

23.   The harp cannot play the notes of a chord simultaneously (hence the term *arpeggio*) but the player will do his best if a chord is marked *sec.* This gives a kind of pseudo-*pizzicato* effect though not quite so dry, and can be useful to 'point' an accent—see ex. 106, bar 6.

24.   Harp tone is distinctly evanescent; it has nothing like the sustaining power of the piano. The *laisser vibrer* effect can be useful:

25.   Quick repeated notes are taken enharmonically on alternate strings—a single string does not repeat clearly at speed. Ex. 101 (*a*) would be played as at (*b*), though the player would probably prefer to see the notation of (*a*).

In such a case the one thing to be remembered is that a D flat would involve an impossibly quick pedal change. Further, such a passage is only possible at certain pitches. The only 'natural' notes which have enharmonics are E, F, B and C.

26.   Glissandos, either up or down, are useful but should not be overdone. Scale glissandos are simple: indicate the setting of the strings and mark the passage *gliss.* If this is done, only the first and last notes need to be actually written:

Arpeggio glissandos involve enharmonics, some notes being taken by two consecutive strings, and it is necessary to be sure that everything can be set to fit. This is always possible with a diminished 7th (ex. 103 (*a*)) and with *some* other 7th chords (*b*); but in many cases some step movement is needed, though it will not show sufficiently to mar the desired effect (*c*).

Ex. 103

In the part, the setting would be indicated in the usual manner, *i.e.* (*a*) would appear as:

B♮, C♭, D♮, E♯, F♮, G♯, A♭

followed by the notation on the lines of ex. 102.

27.   An upward glissando ————— gives a tremendous lift to a climax chord—see ex. 106. Glissando can be used in double notes (3rds, 6ths, octaves) or even in three- or four-part chords, though these last are by way of being rather rare special effects, not to be over-used. For a fine example, see Stravinsky's 'Fire Bird' suite, miniature score page 73, fig. 15.

28.   Harmonics have a clear bell-like tone and sound one octave above written pitch. They are indicated by a small circle (**O**) above the note. They can only be effective either entirely solo or against a very light texture on other instruments. See Elgar's 2nd Symphony, 1st movement, miniature score page 22, fig. 23, where harmonics strike 8 o'clock.

29.   Arpeggio figuration is, naturally, most effective on the harp, with three or four notes to each hand. This kind of thing comes off well:

Ex. 104

30.   The above by no means exhausts the possible uses of the harp, but is as much as is likely to be needed by the elementary student. The rest is to be learned by study of scores, especially those of such composers as Debussy, Ravel and others of the French school, and by consultation with a good player.

EXERCISES

The following are all by Debussy.
1. 2nd Arabesque, for 1 fl., 1 ob., 1 cl., 1 bn., 3 hns., 2 tpts., timp., hp. and strings.
2. 'Children's Corner', "Sérénade à la Poupée", for 2 fl., 1 ob., 2 cl., 1 alto sax., 1 bn., 2 hns., hp., strings without CB.
   The staccato accompaniment will naturally be pizzicato strings.
   Bars 3 to 7 and 9 to 13 offer a pleasing little problem, the difficulty being to get the grace notes, especially in bars 6, 7, 12 and 13, where they are marked to be sustained. One solution is to put the melody in 4ths on two clarinets (bars 3 to 7, resolving on first beat of bar 8) and 2 flutes (bars 9 to 13, resolving on first beat of bar 14), and to double throughout by 4ths on the harp, marking them with the arpeggio sign.
   Note the bottom part melody which begins in bar 15—a nice chance for saxophone, who can also take the inner melody from bar 45. Alternatively this latter would go well on bassoon.
   Bars 115 to 120 can stand as given, on the harp.
   From bar 121 note the marking for the sustaining pedal; think this out carefully.
3. 'Children's Corner', "Jimbo's Lullaby", for 1 C.A., 1 cl., 1 B.Cl., 1 alto sax., 1 bn., 1 D.Bn., 4 hns., timp., hp., strings.
   There are opportunities here for solo use of C.A., B.Cl., sax., and D.Bn. Remember, too, the effect of stopped horns and be prepared to 'create a sustaining pedal' at the top of the second page.
4. 'Children's Corner', "Golliwog's Cake-walk", for full orchestra including B.Cl., D.Bn., S.D., B.D., cym. and hp.
   At the *Cédez* on the third page remember that we have a quotation from Wagner's 'Tristan'. What instrument begins the prelude?
5. 'General Lavine, Eccentric' (Preludes, book 2), for full orchestra, including 3 tpts. but without harp.
   The opening *strident* passages should be on muted tpt. There are some good opportunities for solo bn.
6. 'Hommage à S. Pickwick, Esq.' (Preludes, book 2), for same orchestra.
7. 'Bruyères' (Preludes, book 2), for 2 fl., 2 ob. (2nd changing to C.A.), 2 cl., B.Cl., 2 bn., 4 hns., timp., hp. and strings.

14. Examination Problems

1.   So far we have been concerned with the arrangement of pieces written specifically for the piano, a task involving considerable use of imagination in deciding on the treatment of any given passage. A common type of examination question is that which requires the scoring of a passage which, though given in short score, was conceived by the examiner in more or less orchestral terms. It is therefore not so much a matter of deciding which instrument or instruments will best suit the case at any given point, but rather, which instrument or instruments the examiner had in mind; though the two aspects are in any case largely bound up with each other.

2.   Ex. 105 is a fairly typical example, to be scored for full orchestra, including three trumpets and harp, with piccolo *ad lib.*

Bars 1 to 5. The accompanimental chords, quietly sustained, obviously require homogeneous tone. V.1 and V.2 *div.* look possible until we examine bar 4 (see below). So the solution is horns, whose smooth tone will serve excellently.

Bar 3. Style, pitch and the marking *plaintivo* demand oboe solo.

Bar 4. First reaction may be fl. and cl. soli, but we have to allow for the high 3rds in bar 6, which must obviously be two fl. So bar 4 will be strings.

Bar 6. The *poco sf*—four-part chord—can only be hns., to which we shall add a *sec* chord on hp. to mark the accent. The *staccato* bass *must* be *pizz.* (Students have been known to put it on bn., which betrays a serious lack of aural imagination—it would sound merely silly.)

Bar 7. A solo hn. has the right broad tone for the little tune and the spread bass chords give an opportunity to show that we understand the use of *piano* trb.

Bar 8. This begins the build-up to the climax so the full tone of the strings is essential, with bass chords *pizz.*

Bar 9. The fanfare on the middle stave is obviously tpts. which will carry on into the next bar. Wood-wind are added to help the build-up of tone and the tuba can fatten the bottom octave of the bass.

Bar 10. Last beat, a downward fanfare effect on trb.

Ex. 105

Bar 11. The *marc.* passage on the middle stave gives a chance to use horns *a*4.

Bar 12. More fanfare, passing from trb. to tpt.

The final run up may well be assisted by a harp glissando, and the piccolo will add some glitter.

Notes to ex. 106 : (*a*) Cymbal tap gives an extra touch of colour.

(*b*) Harp fills in quietly, though it could be dispensed with.

(*c*) No need to use more than the one trb.

(*d*) S.D. roll helps the ———— .

(*e*) The high Vc. marks this melodic line well.

(*f*) Oboes add a little edge to horns.

(*g*) Note the tight spacing of the brass here.

(*h*) Note balance of this unison. Flutes omitted—they will add exactly nothing to the effect at this pitch.

Ex. 106

3. As a contrast to the above we will now consider ex. 107, which is based on a style found in certain papers. It is to be scored for double wood-wind, 2 horns, 2 trumpets, timpani and strings.

Ex. 107

This offers very little help. Apart from the obvious horn opening and the suggestion of tpts. and hns. in bars 8 and 9, it is not specifically orchestral and could just as well be a rather uninteresting and unidiomatic bit of piano writing; or merely an example of 'black dots on paper'. It will obviously need a good deal of filling-in at times, and there are no evident solo passages other than those already mentioned. We must remember, too, that since two of each wood-wind instrument are specified, somehow or other we must use them all. The only point in favour of the passage is that it does demand real ingenuity in devising a treatment which will sound reasonably effective, the more since its musical value is (deliberately) practically *nil*.

Ex. 108 shows a possible solution.

The almost unbroken string writing can hardly be avoided, but some attempt has been made to give the wood-wind a little interest.

Ample exercises are to be found in the past papers of the various examining bodies.

Ex. 108

15. Reducing for Small Orchestra

1. The problem here is obviously twofold:
  (*a*) What *must* be kept in?
  (*b*) What *can* be left out?
Broadly speaking the answer is:
  (*a*) Every essential, *i.e.* melody (or melodies) and the fundamental harmonic basis.
  (*b*) Unessential doublings or thickenings of the texture.

2. If the original texture is simple and thin, difficulties are minimised and really only arise when we are not allowed the particular instrument or instruments originally assigned to the passage. If, for example, we have no oboe, a solo for that instrument may have to be transferred to the clarinet; a passage originally for clarinets in 3rds may have to be shared by one clarinet and one oboe; and so on. (Incidentally, it is worth recalling the use of a muted trumpet to substitute for a missing 2nd oboe.)

3. The real difficulties arise in the arrangement of *tutti* passages and it has to be realised that the heavy, massed tone of the true full orchestra cannot be achieved; the sound of the smaller combination is inevitably thinner. More use may need to be made of strings, but even this may need a lot of thought, especially if a definite and limited number of instruments is specified, as in the next paragraph. If we indulge in a lot of *divisi*, there will be no body left in the tone.

4. As a mildly troublesome exercise, we will see what can be done with ex. 106, to be arranged for 1 fl., 1 ob., 1 cl., 1 bn., 1 hn., 1 tpt., four V.1, three V.2, 2 Va., 2 Vc., 1 CB. At first glance this does not look very hopeful, but analysis is instructive. Refer continually to ex. 109.
Bars 1 to 5. Our single horn is useless here and the only possible substitute, to obtain homogeneous tone, is strings. We must, however, allow for the octave passage in bars 4 to 6. This can be on V.1 *div.*, leaving V.2 and Va. for the four-part chords. These will have to be double-stopped since three V.2 *div.* will not balance—two against one.

Bar 3. Oboe solo can stand.

Bar 6. The fl. 3rds must be faked; we could omit the lower notes, but they can easily be taken by oboe. The obvious first choice would seem to be clarinet, but at this pitch it may tend to overbalance the flute.

Bar 7. Solo horn can stand. Trombone chords can only be strings, with bassoon backing up CB.

Bar 8. This can stand except, of course, for the harp.

Bar 9. Our real troubles begin. Strings and wood-wind are simple enough, but what about the brass fanfare? The only thing is to put tpt. at the top, hn. in the middle and trb. at the bottom, and to reduce the 3rd beat chord to three parts, well spaced.

Bars 10/11. The trb. octaves will have to go. One could put hn. on the upper notes and trb. on the lower, but this will rather detract from the effectiveness of the *marcato* hn. in bar 11, which is obviously essential. Trb. solo on the lower octave could serve, but it will be better on the upper notes—the tone is more brilliant. A possible alternative would be to add the lower strings in octaves, but this will detract from the pure brass effect. The solo trb. can do quite well on his own.

Bar 11. There are three melodic lines here; work them out one by one, allowing for octave doubling of the top one.

Bar 12. The troublesome fanfares have to be thinned out a bit. First beat hn. and trb., second beat tpt. and hn. *Note the horn part here*. On the third beat brass have the three upper notes of the V^7, resolving correctly across the barline.

It is not suggested that this is the only possible solution to this problem, but within its inevitable limits it would be effective enough.

Ex. 109

Notes: (*a*) To interlock V.2 and Va. would cause a little trouble over fingering.

(b) The muted 3rd on tpt. and trb. gives pungency to the *sf*.

5.   We may well conclude by a brief discussion of the handling of short extracts from a couple of well-known orchestral works of which the scores should be readily available. These extracts can be taken as fairly typical of the problems encountered in examination papers, requiring reduction from full to small orchestra. It is essential to bear in mind what was said in para. 1 of this chapter.

(i)   Mendelssohn, Italian Symphony, opening of first movement, for 1 fl., 1 ob., 1 cl., 1 bn., 1 hn., 1 tpt. and strings.

V.1 and V.2 obviously remain unaltered, our difficulty being the shortage of instruments for the wood-wind repeated chords. These cannot be thinned out too much or they will lose much of their point. With the hn. we have only five instruments to play with, to which we can add the tpt. at low pitch where it will not obtrude.

Ex. 110

(ii) At the second subject (bar 110, page 11, miniature score) the doubled parallel 3rds (2 clarinets and 2 bassoons) must be retained. Put cl. above ob. for the upper ones and hn. above bn. for the lower. Strings remain as in the original.

(iii) The third movment offers one or two small problems.

    (*a*) Horns, bars 8 to 12. Tpt. can take the upper notes, hn. the lower.

    (*b*) Bars 16 to 20. What are we to do about the low horns here since the upper note is too low for tpt? (It is assumed that the student understands the transpositions clearly.) The simplest solution is for 1st hn. to remain, with bn. taking over 2nd. Note also the arrangement of the cadence bars. Ob. substitutes for fl. 2, hn. takes bn. 1. The D sharp (written F sharp) of 2nd cl. may safely be omitted—V.1 and Va. do all that is necessary.

Ex. 111

After the double bar the lower notes of the oboe octaves will go on clarinet, leaving the oboe tone at the top, where it will show.

(iv) Page 65, miniature score, hns. and bns. need some thought. We cannot achieve Mendelssohn's homogeneous tone unless we transfer to strings, and this would do away with the tone-contrast at the entry of V.1. The solution is hn. at the top (where its characteristic tone will show), bn. at the bottom, and ob. and cl. in between.

Ex. 112

(v) Refer to miniature score page 90 (last movement), four bars before fig. 110. Here we have a knotty problem. With V.1 and V.2 as given, we could use cl. and ob. for the cl. 3rds, but then we are short of an instrument from bar 110 where the fl. enters. The doubling of the fl. melody in 3rds is essential since it has been characteristic throughout the movement; nor can we well eliminate anything from the cl. part here. The possibilities seem to be (a) leave the repeated notes to V.2 and substitute V.1 *div.* for the cl. 3rds, with fl. and ob. entering ar bar 110; (b) use cl. and ob. from bar 106 and V.1 *div.* from bar 110. But in either case we lose some of the 'wind solo' quality. We have, however, a tpt. which, *pp leggiero*, can take cl. 2 at bar 106, leaving fl. and ob. at 110. Hence:

Ex. 113

Notes: (*a*) Cl. and tpt. would work equally well the other way up.

(b) Muted tpt. as 2nd ob. would be good here, but tpt. as 2nd cl. in the opening bars of this example must be open, and there would be no time to put in the mute.

(c) Useful substitute for the pseudo-*pizz.* effect of the off-beat fl. and cl. chords.

(d) Hn. substitutes for 2nd bn.

(e) High B flat shake on 1st ob. is omitted. As laid out here the chord is well
spaced.

(vi) Lack of instruments to provide homogeneous tone in chordal passages often gives trouble. Refer to the opening of the March in Tchaikovsky's 'Casse Noisette' Suite. Despite the use of cl. (doubling tpt.) the overall effect is of a quiet brass fanfare.

Ex. 114

With the orchestra of ex. 113 true homogeneity cannot be achieved, but ex. 115 shows an effective possibility. Tpt. at the top makes the *idea* of brass fairly clear and hn. is consistently on the 3rd of the chord.

Ex. 115   Ob.
Cl. in A
Bn.
Hn. in F
Tpt. in B♭

If we were allowed a piano, the solution would be to give it the whole passage, solo, *i.e.* ex. 114.

(vii) Still more troublesome is the full brass version of the passage, starting in the last bar of page 37, miniature score, with trb. doubling an octave lower. Without a piano it is almost impossible to fake this effectively; we can only open out the spacing and hope for the best, though in any case we shall lose the bite of the original spacing.

Ex. 116   Ob.
Cl. in A
Bn.
Hn. in F
Tpt. B♭

A piano again would be a great help, since ex. 115 could stand with piano taking trb. parts transcribed literally, or else doubling the whole thing in conjunction with the wind.

For suitable exercises the student is again referred to the papers of various examining bodies.

16. The Piano and other Percussion Instruments

1. It is only comparatively recently that the piano has come to be considered for use as a purely orchestral instrument. Early examples may be found in Stravinsky's 'Petrouchka' and Scriabin's 'Prometheus', both of which (especially the latter) require a player of more or less virtuoso technique. For the normal purposes of arranging it is well to be more modest in one's demands. Other examples may be found in Stravinsky's 'Symphony in Three Movements' and Walton's 2nd Symphony.

2. For the composer the virtue of the piano is its percussive character, both solo and in combination with other instruments. For the former see Walton, 1st movement, bars 25 and 28—consider how much less effective these chords would be on the harp. For the latter see bars 127, 130, 132, 134 and 135, and try to realise the effect of the piano's 'clang' superimposed on the tone of the other instruments. As a further example I may perhaps include two short quotations from a work of my own (ex. 117*a* and *b*):

In both cases the piano gives a colour unobtainable by any other means. In full score it may be written immediately above the strings.

Ex. 117

3. For the arranger the piano has three chief uses, (*a*) as a substitute for the harp, (*b*) as a kind of *continuo* and general helper-out in small or none too reliable bands and (*c*) to supply homogeneous tone when it is not otherwise obtainable.

4. (*a*) Two points to be remembered:

   (i) Harp tone, unless the strings are immediately damped by the hands 'hangs on' to some small extent, so discreet use of the sustaining pedal is necessary. Exx. 99 and 104 would both obviously need pedal. Note, too, that in ex. 99 the chord would need to be marked with an arpeggio sign, whether or not it were given in the actual harp part.

   (ii) The piano can only glissando entirely on white notes or entirely on black ones. Scale glissandos involving both white and black notes must often be 'watered down' to achieve playability. Ex. 102, for example, would become something like:

Ex. 118

Note the illusory effect of the low F in the left hand.

(*b*) Use of the piano as general helper-out depends on the other instruments available and the ability of the players. It is not usually necessary to keep the piano going the whole time otherwise the piece may tend to sound too much like a piano solo with orchestral accompaniment. Refer to Mendelssohn's 16th Song without Words. The demisemiquaver arpeggios can only be piano, with 'cellos (and basses) sustaining the low bass notes. In the *forte* passage beginning on the last quaver of bar 4 piano may play as in the original with strings suitably arranged; but at the *piano* at the end of bar 8 strings or wood-wind without piano will be effective provided that the players are reliable enough. And so on.

In some cases the piano may well take over an accompaniment *en bloc*, *e.g.* in the 7th Song without Words, where the opening might score thus:

Ex. 119

Similarly in the 'Spring Song', though a harp would naturally be preferable if available.

Occasionally it is effective to use the piano entirely solo, deliberately exploiting its individual colour. Refer to Grieg's Lyric Pieces, op. 12, no. 4—'Dance of the Elves'. One out of several ways of scoring the opening would be:

Ex. 120

(c) With regard to homogeneity of tone, refer back to chapter 15. Ex. 115 is a fair solution of the problem posed by ex. 114, but piano solo would be more effective. Still more with ex. 116 which could be satisfactorily replaced by:

Ex. 121

Played with a crisp, firm touch and with pedal only on the final chord, this would sound quite adequately brassy. Any available brass and wood-wind could be added if desired, but the piano should be considered as soloist.

5.   For the sake of completeness brief mention now follows of other percussion instruments, though some at least are but rarely encountered.

6.   The *Tenor Drum* (abb. T.D.). In size this lies between the side drum and the bass drum. Having no snares it lacks the rattling tone of the former, nor has it the low booming sound of the latter. Its tone is impressive and dry.

7.   The *Tambourine* (abb. Tamb.). This may be played in three ways:

  (i) by striking the head with the knuckles;
  (ii) by shaking;
  (iii) by rubbing the head with the thumb.

(i) gives a slightly 'drummish' effect plus the tinkle of the jingles;
(ii) gives a 'roll' on the jingles;
(iii) gives a less noticeable roll of the jingles.

The tambourine's usefulness is primarily rhythmical and it can also add a touch of colour.

8. The *Triangle* (abb. Tri.) is rarely of use except in *piano* when in the right context (which must be decided by the use of imagination) its gentle 'tink', or tinkling roll, can be effective enough. It does not come through any big mass of tone, even though some composers seem to expect it to do so. The roll is indicated like one on the side drum and the part can be written in the top space of the percussion stave, clearly marked 'Tri'.

9. The *Glockenspiel* (abb. Glock.).
Compass:

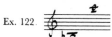

Ex. 122

sounding two octaves higher.

Its bell-like effect can be very useful for touches of colour but should not be over-used. A good example is found in the 'Apprentices' Dance' in the 3rd act of Wagner's 'Meistersinger', miniature score page 403. It can be fairly agile, but do not ask for too much.

10. The *Celesta* (abb. Cel.).
Compass:

Ex. 123

sounding one octave higher.

Like the glockenspiel, whose tone it somewhat resembles though with less sparkle and bite, it should not be over-used. Being a keyboard instrument it has the advantage of great agility, as is shown in the 'Danse de la Fée Dragée' in Tchaikovsky's 'Casse Noisette' Suite. The use that Walton makes of it in his 2nd Symphony is well worth studying.

11. The *Xylophone* (abb. Xyl.).
Compass:

Ex. 124

sounding one octave higher.

Allow for the hard dryness of its tone. In *forte* it can sound pretty clearly through a fair mass of tone, the usual example being in Saint-Saens' 'Danse Macabre'.

The lay-out of the instrument is rather like that of the piano keyboard—'white' notes to the front, 'black' notes to the rear, so that glissandos, either all white-note or all black-note, are possible.

Normally only two sticks are used, but four—two in each hand—are possible, making three- or four-note chords available. High-speed chords are not, however, manageable. Time must be allowed for the player to adjust the spacing (up to about a 5th) and angles of the sticks. This kind of passage is quite practicable:

Ex. 125

12. The *Vibraphone* (abb. Vib.).
Compass:

Ex. 126

written at actual pitch.

The lay-out of the instrument and its technique are similar to those of the xylophone. The tone is amplified by tubular resonators below the metal plates which are struck and the tone dies away gradually. There is an electrically operated mechanism to give *vibrato* (*tremolo*), the speed of which can be varied—and the use of which, at least in 'non-pop' music, should be treated with the greatest reserve. Up to four mallets can be used as on the xylophone.

Examples of the use of the vibraphone are to found in Walton's 2nd Symphony, score pp. 78, 92, 95.

13. *Bells*. Orchestrally they are not bells at all but metal tubes suspended from a frame, struck by a hammer with a rawhide head.
Compass:

Ex. 127

There is a pedal to damp the sound when necessary.

As with so many other instruments, their effectiveness is in inverse proportion to the frequency of their use. For two excellent examples see Delius's 'Brigg Fair' Variations, miniature score pp. 23 and 45.

14. The *Gong* or *Tam-tam*. Pitch is indefinite and effectiveness, again, depends on rarity of use. In the right context its effect can be spine-chilling whether in *piano* or *forte*. For the former see the beginning of the final (C major) section of Strauss's 'Tod und Verklärung'; for the latter the climax of the last movement of Rimsky-Korsakov's 'Scheherezade'.

15.   Chinese (Temple) Blocks. A full set comprises five, of different but indefinite pitches. They may be struck with either a soft mallet or with hard drum sticks. Opportunities for use are rare unless you wish, for example, to try to create a pseudo-Chinese atmosphere—or to imitate horses trotting.

EXERCISES

The following are all from Debussy's Preludes for pianoforte and should give the student ample opportunity to exercise his imagination in the matter of colour.

1. 'Voiles' (book 1), for double wood-wind (Cor Anglais *ad lib.*), 4 horns, glockenspiel or celesta, harp, strings.
2. 'Les sons et les parfums' (book 1), for same orchestra plus timpani.
3. 'La Fille aux Cheveux de Lin' (book 1), for same orchestra.
4. 'Des pas sur la neige' (book 1), for 1 fl., 1 ob., 1 cl., 1 bn., 2 hns., hp., strings.
5. 'Canope' (book 2), for 2 fl., 1 ob., 1 C.A., 2 cl., 2 bn., 2 hn., timp., celesta, hp., strings.
   Note that a good deal of strings *divisi* will be needed.
6. 'Les Collines d'Anacapri' (book 1), for full orchestra including picc., tenor sax., 3 tpts., glock., hp.

At first sight this looks just about impossible since the idiom is super-pianistic; but something can be done with it.

For orchestral purposes Debussy's double time-signature must be discarded. Put bars 1, 2, 5 and 6 in 6/8, also the whole of the middle section bars 49 ff; the rest in 12/16.

Bars 1, 2, 5, 6 obviously hp. but something must be added to help sustain the tone.

Bar 11, etc. Semiquavers on cl. with fl. solo above. Don't give the whole of the semiquavers to one instrument; share them between 1° and 2°.

Bar 21, etc. Semiquavers must become repeated octaves—vas. *div.*

Bar 31, etc. On similar lines (not only vas.)

Bar 49 ff. A nice chance for solo sax. L.H. repeated F sharps will go well on timp.

Bar 68. The chord is marked to be sustained by pedal through three bars, so the *laisser vibrer* effect must be faked in some way. The student may experiment for himself.

Bars 92/93. This may well be doubled completely an octave lower.

Bars 94/95. Debussy's notation here is not helpful though the effect he desires is obvious enough to the pianist. The hemidemisemiquavers are really written-out chords in quick arpeggio, possible (literally) only on the piano or harp at the required speed. Harp is hardly strong enough on its own and we must also allow for the effect of the sustaining pedal. This may be suggested by a high, tightly spaced chord of B major on three tpts., held through to the end. Harp chords, *glissando* with the thumbnail for extra bite, can be backed up by (*a*) pizzicato strings and (*b*) wood-wind.

17. The School Orchestra

1. Any advice offered on scoring for a school orchestra must of necessity be only generalised since such bands vary widely in both composition and ability. The obvious essentials to be borne in mind are that it is no use writing passages which individual players cannot handle and that the total effect should be *musical*. This latter remark may appear superfluous, but one has heard all too often quite horrible noises due to the fact that the arranger has either tried to keep too closely to the original scoring, regardless of balance, or has decided to give something to, say, his solitary oboe or horn just to keep him occupied. Thus an inner part in a passage basically on strings may obtrude unduly, with the wrong kind of tone—and quite possibly badly out of tune as well!

2. The piano, as has been shown in the preceding chapter, is a very present help in time of trouble, but there is no need to use it without intermission—unless, of course, the rest of the band are so weak that they must have continuous support. In which case it would obviously be better to delay performance until they have gained greater ability. The piano can be especially useful on a bass line, since 'cellos and basses are invariably in short supply and their players seem generally to be of a lower standard than those of the violins. For this reason, in such a case as ex. 119 it would probably be as well to include the original bass in the piano part.

3. On account of the scarcity of viola players it is often necessary to divide the available violins into 1sts, 2nds and 3rds.* This causes occasional complications owing to the loss of the lowest 5th of the viola compass. Spacing of chords may have to be revised, or passages which one feels well suited to strings may need to be given to other instruments. Refer to Grieg's Lyric Pieces, op. 12, no. 3, 'The Watchman's Song'. We will assume a band of 1 fl., 1 cl., 1 bn. (unreliable), 1 hn., 1 tpt., 4 V.1, 4 V.2, 4 V.3, 2 Vc., piano.

  The lack of violas presents immediate problems in bars 2 to 4 and 7 and 8. They obviously require tone as nearly homogeneous as possible and in any case strongly suggest

---

* It may be worth mentioning that it is *not* the best thing to put all the good players on V.1, though it is often done. The result is that V.2 and V.3 are inevitably weak and unreliable. They must have a reasonably good player or players to give them a lead.

strings. But violins cannot take the low E's and D sharps. A clarinet or a bassoon could take the 'tenor' line but may spoil the blend. So we must do some re-arranging, thus:

Ex. 128

This, admittedly, loses something of the effect of the original spacing in bars 3 and 4, and 7 and 8, but there is no better way with our limited means. Note that the violins are left undoubled throughout. There is some temptation to have 1st and 2nd violins in unison in bars 1 and 5, but then there will be a sudden weakening of the tone on the top line in bars 2 and 6; besides which it is likely that our two modest 'cellos on the bass line will be overbalanced.

The next phrases suggest a change to wood-wind colour, but we had better let Vc.

assist the unreliable bn. Fl. may well double the melody at the octave in bars 11 and 12, and strings may 'thicken the gravy' to add a little intensity.

Ex. 129

If the horn† is not entirely safe he may be helped by, say, 2nd violins.

So far the piano has not been needed, nor would it be appropriate. At the change of key, however, it must be used for the arpeggios—nobody else can do them. The little fanfares present something of a problem. Tpt. can take the top line, clar. the middle and hn. the bottom. But it will be well to back up with the piano, and by so doing we can get the full four-part semibreve chords.

4.   Refer now to no. 8 of the same suite, the 'National Song', to be scored for 1 fl., 1 ob., 2 cl., 1 bn., 2 tpts., 2 trb., side drum, bass drum, vns. 1, 2, 3, cellos, CB and piano. Bars 1 and 2 and 5 and 6 are obvious—2 trb. What of 3 and 4, 7 and 8? Too low for strings and we have not enough wood-wind for the low pitch, while to raise the pitch

† See para. 6.

an octave would ruin the passages completely. Hence, piano solo. Bars 9 and 10 will suit strings excellently both as regards pitch and colour, and from there to bar 13 we can build up the tone by gradual addition of other instruments.

The temptation in a short piece like this is to score needlessly heavily with the idea of keeping players well occupied. As arranged in ex. 130 there is a fair amount of variety of colour and wood-wind and brass have good practice in counting rests.

Ex. 130   *Maestoso*

5.   In the pieces just considered the piano has been used either for its 'solo' tone or for backing up. We may now take a case where it functions well as a 'continuo'—the Gavotte from Bach's 3rd Orchestral Suite in D major. We will assume the following orchestra:

> 1 fl., 1 ob., 2 cl., 1 bn., 2 tpts., 2 timp., V.1, V.2, V.3, 2 Vc., CB, piano.

A quick glance shows us that in Gavotte I the Va. part can be transferred entirely to V.3. In Gavotte II, however, there are bars which contain notes below violin compass. See ex. 131 (*b*).

Bach's 1st trumpet part has problems owing to its use of high notes, *e.g.* the top (sounding) A in the initial half bar and other places. Since our trumpets will be in B flat this would mean a written top B—distinctly risky with the average school-band player. Be prepared to let him take the A an octave lower.

The oboe parts will be shared with flute and clarinet.

It will be well to work out some dynamic variety; there is no need for unbroken *forte* throughout. Detailed phrasing and bowing are also needed. Ex. 131 shows a suitable working.

6.   As already remarked, there is no need to despise the saxophone if available. Apart from solo work, provided the tone is appropriate, it can substitute quite well for clarinet or bassoon and even more so for horn. Young saxophonists are likely to be more common than young horn players or bassoonists in any case. The little horn part in ex. 129 could quite well be taken by saxophone and would almost certainly be more reliable.

7.   It may be worth remarking that in arranging for a school band (or for any other combination) there is no need to use every available instrument just for the sake of using it. A piece such as Grieg's 'Dance of the Elves', for example, needs no brass at all. The players for whom no part is provided may feel left out in the cold, but they can always take their share in something else.

8.   Finally, let it be stressed again that the aim must be to achieve a good *musical* effect at all costs. However 'scratch' our orchestra may be, this must never be forgotten.

Ex. 131. (A)

(*B*)

ERRATUM

Note: (*a*) If V.2 and V.3 are safe enough, clarinets can be omitted up to the *forte*.

Index